PR4169.B55

D0291930

JE

DATE DUE		
OCT 14 '81		
DEC 1 '82		
NOV 16 '88		
JAN 24 '90		
OCT 23 '91		
APR 06 '94		

Twayne's English Authors Series

Sylvia E. Bowman, *Editor*

INDIANA UNIVERSITY

Charlotte Brontë

TEAS 203

Charlotte Brontë

CHARLOTTE BRONTË

By MARGARET HOWARD BLOM

University of British Columbia

TWAYNE PUBLISHERS
A Division of G. K. Hall & Co.
Boston, Massachusetts, U. S. A.

Library of Congress Cataloging in Publication Data

Blom, Margaret.
　Charlotte Brontë.

　(Twayne's English authors series; TEAS 203)
　Bibliography: p. 169–74.
　Includes index.
　1. Brontë, Charlotte, 1816–1855 — Criticism and
interpretation.
PR4169.B55　　823'.8　　76-42225
ISBN 0-8057-6673-1

FOR MY MOTHER

Contents

About the Author

M. H. Blom received her doctorate from the University of Washington and now teaches at the University of British Columbia. The author of several articles on Charlotte Brontë, Dr. Blom is presently working on a study of minor nineteenth-century women writers.

Preface

Since her death in 1855, Charlotte Brontë's literary importance has been firmly established; the bibliography of both biographical and critical studies devoted to her expands with every passing year. That her novels have remained exciting both to the general reading public and to scholars and critics would have pleased Charlotte, who all her life sought recognition and understanding.

My study of Charlotte Brontë offers extended critical discussion of *The Professor, Jane Eyre, Shirley,* and *Villette*—all of which were written in the last nine years of her life and upon which her literary reputation rests. Though I consider each in its own right, I also attempt to show some of the similarities between these works and between them and her life and the juvenilia she wrote almost compulsively for thirteen years.

Because Charlotte was by her own admission cut off from the literary life of her time and forced to find her subjects in her own personal experience and personal response, my study emphasizes the themes of and the subjective material in the novels, rather than their historical context. Because I agree with the many critics who see Charlotte's overt and poetic treatment of sexual passion as being her great contribution to the novel, I concentrate upon her heroines' sexual dilemmas, which form the focal point of her plots.

Charlotte acknowledged and her critics agree that her central subject is always her own emotional reactions, and so I include a biographical chapter which presents the essential facts of her life and, by means of references to her letters and diary fragments, documents her feelings and thoughts. During her youth, Charlotte wrote hundreds of thousands of words of poetry and prose which not only form the seedbed of the themes that obsessed her, but also bear witness to her increasing control of the writer's craft. I discuss the juvenilia in a chapter which both summarizes the plot lines of this involved saga and also offers a critical commentary on it. Believing that the final authority is the text itself, I quote liberally from the works I discuss in the hope that I may thereby stimulate my readers' critical sensibilities.

MARGARET HOWARD BLOM

University of British Columbia

Acknowledgments

I wish to thank all those who kindly have allowed me to quote from the following copyright materials: *The Shakespeare Head Brontë* by permission of Basil Blackwell and Mott Ltd.; Winifred Gérin's *Charlotte Brontë: The Evolution of Genius*, copyright Oxford University Press 1967, by permission of Oxford University Press; Winifred Gérin's *Five Novelettes* by permission of The Folio Society Ltd.; Fannie E. Ratchford's *The Brontë's Web of Childhood* by permission of Columbia University Press and Russell and Russell. I wish also to thank the Editors of *Criticism* for allowing me to use in altered form material from my article *"Jane Eyre:* Mind as Law Unto Itself," *Criticism*, 15, no. 4, Fall, 1973, by permission of the Wayne State University Press, and the Editors of *Canadian Studies in English* for permission to use in altered form material from my article "Apprenticeship in 'the World Below': Charlotte Brontë's Juvenilia," published in the Fall, 1975, issue. Finally I wish to thank the National Portrait Gallery for permission to reproduce the George Richmond portrait of Charlotte Brontë.

Chronology

1816   Charlotte Brontë born April 21 at Thornton in Yorkshire.

1820   Charlotte's father appointed perpetual curate of Haworth.

1821   September 15, Charlotte's mother dies.

1824   Charlotte and sisters Maria, Elizabeth, and Emily become students at the Clergy Daughters' School, Cowan Bridge.

1825   May, Maria dies; June, Elizabeth dies; Charlotte and Emily return home.

1829   Charlotte begins to write the first accounts of what is to become the saga of Glasstown and Angria.

1831   January, Charlotte enrolls at Miss Wooler's School, Roe Head.

1832   May, completes schooling and returns home to tutor sisters.

1835   July, returns to Roe Head as a teacher.

1838   May, resigns position and returns home.

1842   February, Charlotte and Emily enroll in the *Pensionnat Heger*, Brussels; November, Aunt Elizabeth Branwell's death brings girls home.

1843   January, Charlotte returns to Brussels to teach English and to study.

1844   January, leaves Brussels; Brontë sisters attempt without success to start school.

1846   May, *Poems by Currer, Ellis and Acton Bell* published; *The Professor* completed and offered repeatedly for publication, but without success; August, Charlotte begins *Jane Eyre*.

1847   October, *Jane Eyre* published and acclaimed; December, *Wuthering Heights*, by Emily Brontë, and *Agnes Grey*, by Anne Brontë, published.

1848   June, *The Tenant of Wildfell Hall*, by Anne Brontë, published. September 24, Branwell, the only son of the family, dies; December 19, Emily dies.

1849   May 28, Anne dies. October, *Shirley* published.

1853   January, *Villette* published.

1854   June 29, Charlotte marries A. B. Nicholls.

1855   March 31, Charlotte dies.

1857   March, Mrs. Gaskell's *Life of Charlotte Brontë* published; June, *The Professor* published posthumously.

1925   *The Twelve Adventurers and Other Stories*, a collection of Charlotte's juvenilia, published posthumously.

1931– The nineteen volumes of *The Shakespeare Head Brontë*—the
1938   most complete edition of the works of Charlotte, Emily, Anne, and Branwell—published.

1933   *Legends of Angria*, a collection of Charlotte Brontë's juvenilia, published posthumously.

1971   *Five Novelettes*, a collection of Charlotte Brontë's juvenilia, published posthumously.

CHAPTER 1

Charlotte Brontë's Life

IN his perceptive discussion of Charlotte Brontë, Lord David Cecil suggests that a study of this author's life forms a valuable complement to her novels.

All subjective novelists write about themselves. Nor was Charlotte Brontë an exception. Fundamentally, her principal characters are all the same person; and that is Charlotte Brontë. Her range is confined, not only to a direct expression of an individual's emotions and impressions, but to a direct expression of Charlotte Brontë's emotions and impressions. In this, her final limitation, we come indeed to the distinguishing fact of her character as a novelist. The world she creates is the world of her own inner life; she is her own subject.[1]

Condemned by circumstances to a limited and ultimately reclusive existence, Charlotte derived the rich subject matter of her fiction from a highly imaginative and passionate nature which was stimulated and modified by the ordeals of her daily life. And so an examination of her responses to the events of that life provides insights into the nature of her fictional world.

Like the protagonists of her novels, Charlotte Brontë sought always for recognition. That she achieved her goal is, of course, remarkable because literary fame comes to so very few. But even more amazing, Charlotte Brontë achieved eminence as an author while she endured a life of deprivation, frustration, and tragedy. Desiring knowledge for its own sake and as a means to economic security, she was given—because of the straitened financial circumstances of her family—only minimal formal education. Hating the task of teaching, yet accepting the economic necessity of entering the profession, she attempted to start a private school but received not one application from a prospective student. Convinced of her talent and determined to be an author, she and her two sisters,

13

Anne and Emily, published at their own expense a volume of poetry which sold only two copies. Passionate by nature and imbued with a belief in romantic love, she suffered an agony of frustrated desire for a married man and ultimately married a man she did not love. Deeply attached to her family, she watched her brother and two sisters die; and she found that her long sought for, final success as a novelist, coming at the time of these tragedies, was dust and ashes in her mouth.

Throughout all these years of failure, privation, and pain, Charlotte carried out with courage and kindness the simple duties of daily life: keeping house for her father and her husband and participating in parish affairs as was required of a woman who was the daughter of one clergyman and the wife of another. Moreover, she continued to write; and whether she did so out of stoicism or despair, whether she wrote to escape reality or because her many years as an apprentice author had made composition a habit, her achievement remains unique. Her novels' mere existence makes them a monument to the tenacity of the human spirit.

I *Childhood*

Childhood experience and environment—always formative—were unusually important throughout Charlotte's life; like her brother and sisters she never established a separate home with family of her own but lived until her death with her father at Haworth. The Reverend Patrick Brontë, who outlived his daughter by six years, was a forceful, ambitious, intelligent man who endowed his children with intellectual curiosity and infused both his son Branwell and his daughter Charlotte with his own desire for recognition and success. The child of poor, virtually illiterate, Irish parents, young Patrick Brontë displayed such unusual energy, intelligence, and industry that he attracted the attention of two benefactors: one of them tutored Patrick in the classics and helped him achieve the position of village schoolmaster; the other hired Patrick to tutor his children, instructed him in religion, encouraged him to become a minister, and arranged for him to attend St. John's College, Cambridge.[2]

Having received a bachelor of arts degree in 1806, the young Reverend Patrick Brontë seemed destined for success not only in the church but also in the arts: by 1811 he had been appointed to his own living; and in the same year and again in 1813 and 1815 he had published volumes of poetry. His personal life seemed as hopeful as his professional one, for in 1812, he married pretty, vivacious Maria Branwell, who in the following seven years bore him six children. In 1820, when Charlotte was four years old, he was offered the prestigious living of Haworth; and in this isolated moorland town began a long series of family tragedies when Maria, his beloved wife, died of cancer in 1821.

In the years immediately following the death of his wife, Mr. Brontë made several attempts to remarry; but in 1823, when an old sweetheart refused his proposal, he seemingly surrendered all hopes of finding a mate for himself and a mother for what he described as his *"small* but *sweet* little family";[3] and Elizabeth Branwell, who had come north from Cornwall to care for her dying sister, Maria, and who had remained to run the house, became a permanent resident in her brother-in-law's home.

Perhaps Mr. Brontë was, as Mrs. Gaskell, Charlotte's friend and first biographer, believed, a tyrant whose hatred of finery led him to burn the too-fancy red boots given to his children and whose insistence on plain fare led him to starve his family on a diet of potatoes.[4] Or perhaps he was, as an old servant insisted, "a kind and loving husband and father, kind to all about him."[5] Whatever the case, he was clearly unfitted by grief and temperament to supply a fostering maternal love; and Miss Branwell was neither able nor willing to function as a surrogate mother. A woman of little emotional warmth but of strict Methodist conscience, she accepted the rearing of her motherless nephew and nieces as an onerous duty and performed this self-imposed task by directing the housekeeping and by instructing the girls in needlework from the refuge of a bedroom from which she descended only to "tilt" in argument with her brother-in-law.[6]

Growing up deprived of normal familial love, the children were unusually dependent upon one another for companionship and spontaneous affection. Maria, the eldest daughter, an unusually brilliant and loving child, became the children's source of security as well as her father's main emotional prop. When he emerged—as he infrequently did—from his study, Mr. Brontë conversed with her as with an adult about the issues of the day; and Maria's brother and sisters, separated by their father's social position from the other children of the village, imitated the interests which this adored older sister had imbibed from their father.

All the children read widely and well; but if reading offered them a vicarious escape from the Haworth parsonage, it offered no escape from their father's influence, since his tastes and interests dictated which newspapers, magazines, and books came to the house. Left to their own amusement, the young Brontës immersed themselves in the exciting social and political happenings of the day, and the fact that one of Charlotte's earliest memories concerned fervid family discussions of the Catholic Emancipation Bill[7] reveals the degree to which the family was intrigued by contemporary issues. Allowed access to their father's small library, the children also ranged freely through such books as *The Arabian Nights* and John Bunyan's *The Pilgrim's Progress*; they devoured the works of the Romantic poets, including even what was at the time considered the shocking poetry of Lord Byron. Such disparate sources fostered the children's creative talents by providing the basis for a fantasy life so rich and powerful that none of the Brontës ever wholly escaped from it. Their wide reading became yet another bar in their prison of isolation, for it endowed them with a body of odd facts and fantastic ideas which set them apart from other children and made them a puzzle to their teachers, who found them deficient in certain rudimentary skills but unnaturally advanced in other kinds of learning.

It is little wonder that children reared in such bizarre circumstances found their transition to the world beyond the Haworth parsonage difficult, if not impossible. Indeed, the tragedy which overtook the two oldest daughters when they left Haworth can be traced back directly to their formative years at home. In January, 1824, a school for the daughters of poor clergymen opened; and in July of that year—when Maria was ten and Elizabeth was nine—Mr. Brontë availed himself of the opportunity for his children to receive a formal education. Unfitted both physically and mentally for a spartan, intellectually rigid school life, both girls were unhappy away from home; and both Charlotte and Emily, who enrolled in the school later in the same year, witnessed their older sisters' sufferings and the onset of their fatal illnesses.

Whether or not *Jane Eyre's* description of events at Lowood School is an accurate account of life at the Clergy Daughters' School at Cowan Bridge, Charlotte nevertheless believed that she spoke the truth in her novel, and her belief seems to some extent to be substantiated by the facts as we know them. Weakened by bouts with chicken pox, whooping cough, and measles during the previous year,[8] Maria and Elizabeth were surely less able than most children to survive the privations of a charity school. Accustomed to mental freedom at home but deficient in systematic learning and unused to the formal discipline of community life, the elder girls suffered the humiliation of finding that their peculiar brilliance and knowledge were insufficient compensations for their "faults" of daydreaming and poor housewifery. Maria's lot was especially hard; formerly the intellectual companion of her father, she became a scapegoat, suffering the systematic persecution of one Cowan Bridge teacher who, when the child was dying of tuberculosis and barely able to rise from her bed, accused her of "dirty and untidy habits"[9] and forced her to carry on normal school activities.

Maria—like Helen Burns, whom Charlotte created in her image—bore this treatment with a "Christ-like" stoicism,[10] and when she died at home on May 6, 1825, her grieving father recorded that "she exhibited during her illness many symptoms of a heart under divine influence."[11] Then, in the last weeks of May, Elizabeth fell ill, was sent home, and died within two weeks of her return. Mr. Brontë, frightened by the double tragedies, immediately removed Charlotte and Emily from the school,[12] but the experience had left its mark. For the remaining Brontë children, the world beyond Haworth had become threatening and dangerous; never again were any of them to feel wholly safe or happy outside the confines of their home, which had now become a refuge.

Especially for Charlotte, the Cowan Bridge experience was traumatic. Although a former teacher remembered that Charlotte was herself a "general favourite" at school,[13] she had at eight years of age already assumed the "grave" demeanor she wore as an adult; for as she herself explained, "I suffered to see my sisters perishing." The child one of her teachers remembered as "a bright, clever, happy little girl"[14] early formed the outlook of the woman Mrs. Gaskell described as constitutionally devoid of hope.[15] With the death of her sisters, Charlotte became the eldest child of the family, with all the attendant responsibilities of that position, in addition to which she also assumed the burden of attempting to become another Maria, who was deified in her memory. A friend who first met her when she was in her teens recollected that Charlotte's "love for [her dead sisters] was most intense; a kind of adoration dwelt in her feelings";[16] and as an adult, Charlotte remembered Maria's "prematurely-developed and remarkable intelligence, as well as the mildness, wisdom, and fortitude of her character."[17]

Assuming it was now her task to realize the family's ambitions, Charlotte took her new position seriously. Her first duty was to become educated so that she might teach her younger sisters and eventually support herself. In 1831, when she was not quite fifteen, she was again sent away to school—this time to Roe Head, owned and run by the Misses Wooler—and although she was miserably homesick and shy, she displayed the stoicism which was the hallmark of her character and which was also to be so marked a quality of her heroines. When she left Roe Head in 1832, at the end of three terms of schooling, she had not only established the friendships with Mary Taylor and Ellen Nussey that were to last throughout her life, but she had so won the respect of all her schoolmates and teachers that she was presented with a silver medal for "the fulfilment of duties."[18]

II *Angria Versus Duty*

Glad to return home, Charlotte conscientiously devoted her next three years to teaching Emily and Anne. But lessons and housework occupied only part of her time: in her leisure she continued her childhood habit of collaborating with Branwell on a series of tales and poems about an imaginary kingdom on the west coast of Africa. These writings, the Brontë juvenilia, form a complex saga that is exciting in its own right and that is also revelatory of Charlotte's literary and psychological development.

The story of the children's involvement in this sustained fantasy is interesting in itself. In 1829 Charlotte, Branwell, Emily, and Anne—who had long told one another stories about twelve toy soldiers whom they had endowed with names and personalities— began to write down their fantasies, slowly evolving a story of conquest, civil war, involved familial relationships, personal jealousies, loyalties, and loves. While Charlotte was a student at Roe Head, Emily and Anne broke away from chronicling life in what the children called the Glasstown Confederacy and began to record happenings in their own imaginary kingdom of Gondal. Branwell, however, carried on in Charlotte's absence by embellishing and expanding the Glasstown story and by faithfully informing his sister of each new twist and turn of the plot. Homesick and missing the stimulation afforded by her brother's and sisters' creative talents, Charlotte eagerly awaited each new bulletin from Glasstown; and when freed from Roe Head, she renewed with delight her contributions to the unfolding story which now began to center more and more on Angria—a newly created nation within the Glasstown Confederacy.

But despite the engrossing pleasure Charlotte experienced when she wrote, she was not comfortable with her abundant creative abilities: she knew that the practical result of indulging her imaginative powers was negligible. As a schoolgirl, she confessed to one of her schoolmates, Mary Taylor, that she and her brother wrote for each other's amusement, chronicling the adventures of imaginary heroes and heroines in tiny, handprinted volumes that simulated the look of the periodicals of the day. The commonsensical Mary replied that the children "were like growing potatoes in a cellar," and Charlotte had sadly acquiesced, saying, "Yes! I know we are!"[19] Aware of the futility of her creative efforts and of the family's financial need, Charlotte felt burdened with a sense of time passing and time wasted; and in April, 1835, when she was offered an opportunity to return to Roe Head as a teacher and bring with her one of her sisters as a student, she gratefully accepted the position. To Mary Taylor, she "confessed it was not brilliant, but what could she do?"[20] To Ellen Nussey, she remarked that she was "sad, very sad, at the thoughts of leaving home but *Duty—Necessity*—these are stern mistresses who will not be disobeyed."[21]

The letters in which Charlotte announced her resolution indicate the beginning of a long period of suffering in which she sought to satisfy the demands of pragmatic necessity and her own conscience by stifling the compulsive urgings of her creative imagination. Unfitted for teaching by both her extreme shyness and her impatience with the stupidity and lack of interest of her students, Charlotte's misery in her new role was increased by the fact that her awareness of her expanding imaginative powers made her feel that teaching was not only drudgery but an activity which barred her from the only joy she had—that of recording the adventures of the creatures of her fancy. How fully these adventures had preoccupied her while she was at home and free to indulge in fantasy can be gauged by the mass of material she composed: the four volumes which remain of the twelve she wrote in 1833—the year she returned home—average more than twenty thousand words apiece,[22] but this spate of composition abruptly halted when she returned to

teach at Roe Head, since the daily tasks that she hated filled her
time and blocked the flow of her imagination.

The heroes and heroines about whom she had written so copi-
ously seemed to her to exist in a world she had imagined but from
which she was self-exiled by her own sense of responsibility—"I
cannot write of them; except in total solitude, I scarce dare think of
them,"[23] she wrote in her private journal—yet sometimes, almost
unbidden, they came thronging before her mind's eye. An entry of
August 11, 1836, epitomizes the misery engendered by the collision
between sober reality and intoxicating dream:

All this day I have been in a dream half miserable and half ecstatic miserable
because I could not follow it out uninterruptedly, and estatic because it
showed almost in the vivid light of reality the ongoings of the infernal world.
I had been toiling for nearly an hour with Miss Lister, Miss Marriott and
Ellen Cook striving to teach them the distinction between an article and a
substantive. The parsing lesson was completed, a dead silence had succeeded it in the school-room and I sat sinking from irritation and weariness
into a kind of lethargy. The thought came over me am I to spend all the best
part of my life in this wretched bondage, forcibly suppressing my rage at the
idleness and apathy and the hyperbolical and most assinine stupidity of
those fat-headed oafs and on compulsion assuming an air of kindness patience and assiduity? . . . Then came on me rushing impetuously all the
mighty phantasm that we had conjured from nothing to a system strong as
some religious creed. I felt as if I could have written gloriously—I longed to
write . . . if I had had time to indulge it I felt that the vague sensations of
that moment would have settled down into some narrative better at least
than anything I ever produced before. But just then a Dolt came up with a
lesson. I thought I should have vomited. . . .[24]

School holidays were an oasis in the desert of Charlotte's existence; and during these times of freedom, her imaginative powers
assumed full sway, bursting forth energetically in stories and novel-
las, but she could think of no way to put these productions to practical account. During the Christmas holiday of 1836, in an attempt to
obtain a professional writer's evaluation of her work, she sent a
sample of her poetry to Robert Southey; but his response some two
and a half months later, although kind, poisoned her dreams of
balancing the claims of a warm, vital imagination with cold,
economic necessity. Had Southey known the circumstances and the
character of his correspondent, he could not more effectively have
driven the iron into Charlotte's breast; for in Charlotte's eyes, his

rejection of her manuscript denied her the hope that she might someday make money writing and so doomed her to a lifetime of teaching. More terrible yet, his letter implied that it was perverse of her to aspire "to celebrity": "Literature [he said] cannot be the business of a woman's life, and it ought not to be." Moreover, he condemned the perfervid nature of her imagination, warning her that "the day dreams in which you habitually indulge are likely to induce a distempered state of mind; and, in proportion as all the ordinary uses of the world seem to you flat and unprofitable, you will be unfitted for them without being fitted for anything else."[25]

Southey's advice was particularly upsetting because it reiterated Charlotte's own self-condemning appraisal of her writing; for as she had grown older and had become aware of how irresistibly she was attracted to it, she had grown increasingly distrustful of the imaginative world she had created. Drawn to her fantasy kingdom like an addict to his drug, and half despising the escape from reality that she was driven to seek, she was torn by ambivalent impulses which were the product of the influence of romanticism and Protestant Christianity on her early years. Reared by a clergyman who, whatever his personal failings, was a committed Christian, and by Aunt Branwell, who was a fundamentalist Methodist, Charlotte grew up familiar not merely with basic Christian doctrine but also with the idiosyncratic beliefs of various sects, her knowledge of which filled her schoolmates with "wonder."[26]

Although Charlotte was a staunch member of the Church of England, her Calvinist leanings encouraged religious depression;[27] and this tendency to melancholia—which also infected her brother and sisters—was fortified by the fact that all four children were plagued by ill health and lived adjacent to the churchyard where the graves of their mother and two sisters were seen daily from the windows of the parsonage. Accordingly, the Brontë children felt that a dark eternity overshadowed their lives and that salvation depended upon "rejection of the world, the flesh, and the devil."

But Charlotte was also a product of the Romantic Age. The novels of Sir Walter Scott and the poetry of Lord Byron delighted her; and as a child, she had spent many evenings listening to the stories told by Tabby, an old Yorkshire servant, about ghosts and demons or about rejected lovers who either died of grief or flew into murderous rage as a result of betrayal. Charlotte's fiery nature not only drew her to romance and passion but also colored her imagination when she set about delineating the tempestuous lives of the men and women of the Glasstown Confederacy.

The fact that both Branwell and Charlotte referred to their Angrian creation as the "infernal world" and the "world below" gives some indication of the moral judgment they passed upon the substance of their fantasies. For Charlotte, who struggled to live in terms of the Christianity that she professed, the creative impulse became associated with guilt: she sought relief from the drudgery of her everyday life by escaping to the Angria of her imagination; but the very desire to escape—and her awareness that the world which welled up within her and to which she escaped was amoral and violent—became evidence in her eyes of her innately wicked character. In the agonized letters she sent in 1836 to Ellen Nussey, her old schoolmate, she never revealed that she was writing at all or divulged a single detail of her Angrian fantasies, but she spoke again and again of her weakness and her sinful imaginings:

My darling if I were like you I should have my face Zionward . . . but I am *not like you*. If you knew my thoughts; the dreams that absorb me; and the fiery imagination that at times eats me up and makes me feel Society as it is, wretchedly insipid, you would pity and I dare say despise me. But Ellen I know the treasures of the Bible I love and adore them I can *see* the Well of Life in all its clearness and brightness; but when I stoop down to drink of the pure waters they fly from my lips as if I were Tantalus.[28]

Charlotte's Angrian heroines are helpless to stifle their passion for Zamorna—Charlotte's great, romantic hero—although it frightens them and yields only agony. Like her heroines, Charlotte was in love with what she feared; but the compelling and dangerous object of her affection was no human being but imagined men and women who at times usurped her conscious mind, blotting out the claims of conscience with a totality that frightened her. In a journal entry of 1836, she speaks of how "the toil of the day succeeded by this moment of divine leisure had acted on me like opium and was coiling about me a disturbed but fascinating spell such as I never felt before. What I imagined grew morbidly vivid." Impression succeeds impression:

A thousand things were connected with [the vision], a whole country, statesmen and Kings, a Revolution, thrones and princedoms subverted and reinstated—meantime the tall man washing his bloody hands in a bason and the dark beauty standing by with a light remained pictured in my mind's eye with irksome and alarming distinctness. I grew frightened. . . . At last I became aware of feeling like a heavy weight lying across me. I knew I was wide awake and that it was dark and that the ladies were now come into the room to get their curl-papers they perceived me lying on the bed and I heard them talking about me. I wanted to speak, to rise it was impossible—I felt that this was a frightful predicament . . . I must get up I thought and I did so with a start. I have had enough of morbidity and vivid realisations—every advantage has its corresponding disadvantages—tea's ready Miss Wooler is impatient. . . . [29]

The tension between Charlotte's desire to write and her fear of and guilt over submitting to this desire was coupled with her great unhappiness at being constantly compelled to do work she hated and for which she was temperamentally unsuited. The final result was a mental agony so severe that in the spring of 1838, Charlotte suffered a physical breakdown which forced her to resign her position at Miss Wooler's school. When she returned home, she was made yet more miserable by her sense that she had failed even at the inglorious job of school teaching; but since her failure brought her the freedom to write, she continued with a guilty delight to compose sketches and poems about Angria during the following year. Nothing in her situation had changed, however; and in the spring of 1839, feeling restored in health but still driven by economic need, she again forced herself to seek employment, this time as a nursery governess.[30] The misery she suffered during her two months' employment was intensified by her awareness that the position, unpleasant in itself, could lead to nothing but more drudgery.

Her dismissal from this position offered another welcome respite, but one which she knew could be only temporary because of her family's financial prospects. Far from fulfilling his early promise, Branwell had drifted from occupation to occupation; and he now seemed more than likely to become a constant burden on, rather than a support to, his sisters. Emily's one attempt to support herself as a schoolmistress had placed her in a position Charlotte had described as slavery,"[31] and she had returned home with the acquiescence of her sisters, who believed she could not survive away from the freedom of the moors. Mr. Brontë was aging; and since his living would die with him, he would leave his children without a home. Thus in late 1840 and in the spring of 1841, when Anne and Charlotte began a new and diligent attempt to find employment as governesses, they were driven by need.

After a long search, Charlotte again established herself in a position which she disliked but which she retained by sheer force of will. She had gone to her new employers, hoping for little, but determined to succeed. In a letter written to Ellen Nussey shortly after accepting this commitment, Charlotte remarked, "My earnest wish and endeavour will be to please [my employers]. . . . But no one but myself can tell how hard a governess's work is to me—for no one but myself is aware how utterly averse my whole mind and nature are to the employment. Do not think that I fail to blame myself for this, or that I leave any means unemployed to conquer this feeling."[32] Unhappy herself, she also suffered for Anne, now also a governess: "I have [she wrote to Ellen] one aching feeling at my heart . . . —it is about Anne— . . . when my thoughts turn to her—they always see her as a patient, persecuted stranger. . . ."[33]

But no matter how unpleasant teaching was to her and her sisters, it remained their inevitable lot as unmarried girls of no fortune; and in an effort to solve the problems facing them all, Charlotte convinced her sisters that they should open a school of their own and by this means become self-supporting without undergoing the pain of separating themselves from each other. Since this plan required that they improve their qualifications by increasing their knowledge of modern languages, Charlotte and Emily enrolled in February, 1842, in the *Pensionnat Heger*, Brussels, where they could gain greater facility in French and learn German.

III *Brussels and M. Heger*

Older than the other pupils and separated from their concerns by religion and nationality, Emily and Charlotte suffered from homesickness which was mitigated for Charlotte by her delight in using her mental capacities to the full. Writing to Ellen from Brussels, she says, "I was twenty-six years old a week or two since, and at this ripe time of life I am a schoolgirl, a complete schoolgirl, and, on the whole, very happy in that capacity. It felt very strange at first to submit to authority instead of exercising it . . . , but I like that state of things. I returned to it with the same avidity that a cow, that has long been kept on dry hay, returns to fresh grass. Don't laugh at my simile. It is natural to me to submit, and very unnatural to command."[34] Her intelligence and her eagerness to learn won Charlotte the approbation of Monsieur and Madame Heger; and in July, they offered the sisters an opportunity to continue their studies for

another half year in exchange for Emily's services as a music teacher
and for Charlotte's as a teacher of English. This situation, so satisfactory to Charlotte, ended in November when the sisters were called
home by the fatal illness of their aunt. Always unhappy in Brussels,
Emily decided to remain at Haworth to keep house for her father;
but Charlotte, who was warmly urged by the Hegers to return,
again departed for Belgium in January, 1843, to continue her studies
and to resume her position as teacher, which was now offered to her
with a salary as well as with the promise of free lessons.

This decision led to severe misery for Charlotte: without Emily's
companionship, she was intensely lonely and came to depend for
happiness upon Professor Heger, who showed interest in her as a
pupil and to whom she now gave private lessons in English. Heger
was a famous and talented teacher, a devout Catholic, and a devoted
family man; but Charlotte—victimized by her inexperience, her
need, and her imagination—saw him as an Angrian male: enigmatic,
passionate, and brilliant. That Charlotte with her iron self-control
and her fervent desire to live a Christian life could ever have consciously intended to enter into an illicit relationship with a married
man is impossible, but it is also clear that she lost herself in sexual
fantasies about her employer. Madame Heger, discerning Charlotte's growing emotional dependence on her husband, became
coldly formal; Charlotte, increasingly isolated and lonely, became the
victim of her dreams.

The disastrous train of her thought is apparent in a letter to Branwell in which she described the misery occasioned by her discovery
that the inhabitants of the school "are very false in their relations
with each other." Heger alone, she believed, had not betrayed her
friendship, but with him she now had "little or nothing to do,"
although she was "indebted . . . for all the pleasure or amusement
[she] had" to his "kind-heartedness by loading [her] with books."
The nature of this solitary amusement and its dangerous potential is
apparent in the last paragraph of the same letter: having spoken of
her "stagnant, silent life," she announces, "It is a curious metaphys-
ical fact that always in the evening when I am in the great dormitory
alone, . . . I always recur as fanatically as ever to the old ideas, the
old faces, and the old scenes in the world below."[35] But those old
scenes and old faces were now subtly changed; for reality and dream
had mingled, and the phantom-hero of her Angrian stories,
Zamorna, seemed incarnated in M. Constantine Heger.

The English friends in Brussels who had offered her some companionship had left town; and during the long vacation of five weeks, Charlotte lived virtually alone in the echoing halls of the *Pensionnat*. Her depression and loneliness, recounted as the experience of Lucy Snowe in *Villette*, brought about a psychological and spiritual crisis; but Charlotte doggedly remained in Brussels, the prey of increasing despair. Finally in December, urged by Mary Taylor, to whom she confessed her suffering, although probably not its cause, Charlotte resigned her position. On January 1, 1844, she left Brussels for home.

Haworth, however, seemed no longer a refuge but a prison. Her father's increasing dependence upon her, the result of incipient blindness, made it impossible for her to accept a teaching position for which her studies in Brussels had qualified her, and her attempts to start her own school led to nothing: the carefully prepared prospectus sent to friends to announce the opening of "The Misses Brontë's Establishment for the Board and Education of a limited number of Young Ladies [at] the Parsonage, Haworth" resulted in no applications at all. However much she desired "active exertion—a stake in life,"[36] she was totally stymied. "I can hardly tell you how time gets on at Haworth," she wrote to Ellen. "There is no event whatever to mark its progress. . . . Meantime life wears away. I shall soon be thirty, and I have done nothing yet. Sometimes I get melancholy at the prospect before and behind me. . . . I feel as if we were all buried here. I long to travel, to work, to live a life of action."[37]

Bereft of any occupation and obsessed with memories of Brussels that were interwoven with the Angrian fantasies which had long been the channel of her suppressed emotional life, she poured out her feelings in a series of impassioned letters to M. Heger. Appalled by the near-hysterical tone with which she begged for his interest and affection, he first replied to her coldly, then not at all. In desperation, Charlotte continued to write to him, describing the sick agony of spirit with which she waited for letters that never came. The crisis of 1844–1845 was catalytic, for Charlotte's relationship with Heger was only too similar to her Angrian fantasies; and the merging of dream and reality forced her to come to terms with aspects of her personality which earlier she had consciously tried to deny.

In 1839 she had repudiated her muse, saying, "I long to quit for awhile that burning clime where we have sojourned too long—its skies flame—the glow of sunset is always upon it—the mind would cease from excitement and turn now to a cooler region where the dawn breaks grey and sober, and the coming day for a time at least is subdued by clouds."[38] Motivated by guilt, she had consciously chosen to quit Angria so that she might succeed in the workaday world, and to ensure her success in this endeavor, she had gone to Brussels to improve her qualifications for teaching. In Brussels, however, Angrian fantasies still stirred her imagination; and even more ominously, they began to color her perception of the reality about her. What earlier she had feared and refused to write about, she now began to live. Previous guilt over the nature of her fantasies became guilt over her motives and actions where Heger was concerned. As Ratchford notes, the agonized appeals with which in 1844 and 1845 she bombarded Heger, she had written before when she had described the sufferings of Zamorna's abandoned wife, Mary Percy.[39] The passion and the feeling which had infused her imaginative depiction of unrequited love in Angria were now evoked by the situation in which she actually found herself.

Perhaps the horror of discovering in her own life what she had before only imagined totally paralyzed for a time her creative powers: she later admitted to Ellen, "I returned to Brussels after Aunt's death against my conscience—prompted by what seemed then an irresistible impulse—I was punished for my selfish folly by total withdrawal for more than two years of happiness and peace of mind . . .";[40] and during these two years, she wrote no more romances. To Heger, she wrote of "the lethargy of [her] faculties," insisting, "I should not know this lethargy if I could write";[41] and she also insisted to him that her failing eyesight kept her from making a start on a book, an explanation which the context of her statements and her subsequent career suggest was rationalization rather than fact.

Yet the two years of agony, during which time she protested again and again her inability to write, transformed Charlotte and ultimately freed her to make use of creative faculties she had once attempted to stifle and then for a time had found herself unable to evoke. For during this period Charlotte apparently made the momentous discovery that she could turn her passionate, imagina-

tive nature to practical account by utilizing it to describe not obsessive fantasies of an imaginary West African kingdom but real English
landscapes drawn with conscious artistry and peopled by real men
and women who suffered—just as Charlotte suffered—the contradictory demands of conscience and imagination. During two
years of brooding despair, Charlotte learned the most valuable lesson that comes with self-knowledge: she learned to see herself in
others; to identify within herself the sources of others' suffering; and
to create portraits in words of heroes and heroines who, like her,
endured the contradictory demands of self and society, personal
impulse and conscience.

IV   *Triumph and Tragedy*

The process by which Charlotte was eventually able to escape
from the enervating effects of self-reproach and black despair, to
harness her creative impulse, and to become a successful novelist
was slow—marked at first by professional disappointment and then
by great personal grief. In 1845, still suffering from deep depression
and from a fear of blindness, which for a year and a half condemned
her to an aimless existence at Haworth, Charlotte discovered a mass
of Emily's poetry that was of such surprising excellence that it
refired her own literary ambitions. Charlotte had preserved many of
her own poems; and under urging, Anne admitted that she too was
writing poetry. Excited and enthusiastic, Charlotte now convinced
her sisters that they should use part of their aunt's small legacy to
publish a volume of poetry. Partly to protect themselves from prejudice against women writers, partly to meet Emily's demands for
anonymity, the girls used pseudonyms; and the slim volume of
sixty-one poems which appeared in May, 1846, was titled *Poems by
Currer, Ellis and Acton Bell*.

The very ease with which the dream of publication became reality
may have inspired all three sisters to write with more serious purpose. Even while they were involved in settling the details of format
and publicity for their first book, all were hard at work on novels;
and this renewed creative activity helped Charlotte to accept dis-
passionately the failure of their initial attempt to win success as
authors. By the middle of July, despite several complimentary reviews, only two copies of their poems had been sold,[42] but by the
end of June, Charlotte had completed *The Professor;* Emily,
Wuthering Heights; and Anne, *Agnes Grey*. The sisters busied

themselves finding a publisher who would offer all three novels in the then popular three-volume format.

In Charlotte's first novel, although she had used an Angrian character as her hero, she attempted to eradicate all romance from his story. Determined that her protagonist "should work his way through life as I had seen real living men work theirs . . .," she created—as she admitted in the preface—a work deficient in the "imaginative and poetical." Ironically, the desperation which increasing family difficulties caused Charlotte to feel that summer may have contributed to her eventual literary success by adding the emotional power lacking in *The Professor* to the new novel she now began, *Jane Eyre*. Her father, nearly seventy, was going blind; although he was able to carry on his duties with the aid of a curate, total blindness would force him to resign his living, the family's only economic support.

In August, driven by necessity and fearing what might be the outcome, Charlotte and her father went to Manchester where he was to undergo a cataract operation: Emily and Anne remained at home to care for Branwell, who had become an alcoholic and a drug addict. The triple manuscript of *The Professor*, *Wuthering Heights*, and *Agnes Grey* had already been rejected by one publisher—every door to opportunity seemed firmly closed—but in a Manchester boardinghouse, watching her father's slow and uncertain recovery, Charlotte began a new manuscript. Desperate to fill the lonely hours and no doubt eager to block out melancholy reality, she wrote almost without ceasing for three weeks, creating, as if she were under a spell, the story that was to become *Jane Eyre*.

Although the cataract operation was a success, a year of discouragement followed for the sisters; during that time three more publishers refused their three manuscripts. In July, 1847, Charlotte, the most ambitious of the lot, suffered bitter disappointment when Thomas Cautley Newby accepted *Wuthering Heights* and *Agnes Grey*, but refused *The Professor*. Yet even this blow to her pride could not deflect Charlotte from her purpose: her creative impulse—long blocked by guilt and despair—had been freed, and she continued to work on the novel begun almost a year earlier. Thus when early in August she received a sixth rejection of *The Professor*, now going its rounds in solitude, she did not despair; instead, she found encouragement in the fact that the publisher's reader "discussed its merits and demerits so courteously . . . [and]

with a discrimination so enlightened." He had added that if the author wished to submit "a work in three volumes" to his firm— Smith, Elder and Company—it "would meet with careful attention."[43] Charlotte responded at once, saying that she had nearly completed such a work. On August 24, 1847, she posted the hurriedly finished manuscript of *Jane Eyre;* and this novel, in which the blend of Angrian materials and personal experience was suffused with great emotional power, so captivated Mr. William Smith Williams—the reader who had reacted sympathetically to *The Professor*—that he took it immediately to Mr. George Smith, the head of the publishing firm, who experienced similar excitement. The book was accepted at once; published a month and a half later, on October 16, 1847, it won immediate acclaim.

Charlotte's dream now seemed realized—the five hundred pounds she received from her publishers represented economic success; the many complimentary reviews of the book proved her power to please an audience. Her sisters also reaped the benefit of her triumph; for Newby, who had not yet published their novels, capitalized on Charlotte's use of the pseudonym "Currer Bell" and rushed *Wuthering Heights* by "Ellis Bell" and *Agnes Grey* by "Acton Bell" into print, in the hope that *Jane Eyre*'s popularity would gain readers for these other works. The fall and winter of 1847 and the spring and summer of 1848 were, perhaps, the happiest time the three girls had ever known. They read the reviews of their books aloud to one another, and each began a new work.[44] Success and happiness seemed at last assured.

But the sisters' pleasure was short-lived: Branwell, from whom the sisters had hidden the fact that they had ever published anything, continued his physical, mental, and emotional decline; and on September 24, 1848—after a violent illness of only a few days— he died. Although he had long been a misery and a burden to his family, the death of this once so loved and so promising brother was a severe shock. Charlotte responded by falling into an illness which kept her from attending his funeral, which was held in a drizzling rain. Emily who attended, caught a cold which rapidly developed into galloping consumption. Weak from the day of her birth like all the Brontë children, she now sped toward death. Refusing to accept medical advice, she attempted to ignore her increasing debility, stoically carried on her usual activities, and insisted that no account be taken of her illness. Charlotte bore the terrible burden of helplessly watching a loved sister die, and her letters of this time bespeak an agony almost too great to be borne. Writing to Ellen Nussey on November 28, she insisted, "I hope still—for I *must* hope—she is dear to me as life. . . ."[45] Two weeks later, on the morning of December 19, when hope was gone, Charlotte cried out in a second letter to Ellen, "Moments so dark as these I have never known. I pray for God's support to us all."[46] By two o'clock on the afternoon of this same day, Emily was dead: "the anguish of seeing her suffer [was] over."[47]

The intensity of Charlotte's grief was overwhelming, and she begged Ellen to come to her not only to help her endure this pain but also to give her strength to bear the piercing sorrow which, as she foresaw, was yet to come. Always delicate and sickly, Anne had all that fall been suffering from symptoms which were terrifyingly like Emily's. Early in January, a doctor was called; and having examined the patient, he pronounced her to be fatally ill. Yet Charlotte continued to hope—daring nothing else. She felt "like one crossing an abyss on a narrow plank—a glance round might quite unnerve";[48] and she knew that others depended upon her strength. Writing to Ellen immediately after Emily's death, she had said, "My father says to me almost hourly, 'Charlotte, you must bear up—I shall sink if you fail me.' These words . . . are a stimulus to nature. . . . Somebody *must* cheer the rest."[49]

Now she "cherished [Anne] with all the fostering strength" she had, attempting, as she said, to "avoid looking forward or backward, and . . . to keep looking upward. This is not the time to regret, dread, or weep. . . . The days pass in a slow, dark march."[50] Anne—as patient and as quiescent in her illness as Emily had been stoical in hers—slowly sank. In a desperate effort to prolong her sister's fading life, Charlotte, accompanied by Ellen, took Anne to Scarborough, which she longed to see again. But nothing could now avail: leaving Haworth on May 24, the three women arrived at Scarborough on the 25, where the dying Anne peacefully awaited her death, which came calmly on the morning of May 28.

Charlotte returned to the lonely parsonage and to her sorrowing father. In the black days that followed, she continued to work on the novel she had begun to write in the happy summer of 1848 and which she had worked on only sporadically during the intervening period. Three months after Anne's death—by August 29, 1849—she had finished *Shirley*. This book, written as it was during her sisters' illness, was an agony for Charlotte to complete; and perhaps she did so simply because writing had become her only escape from total despair. In a letter to her publishers, she summed up her situation: "How should I be with youth past—sisters lost—a resident in a moorland parish where there is not a single educated family? In that case I should have no world at all: the raven, weary of surveying the deluge and without an ark to return to, would be my type. As it is, something like a hope and motive sustains me still."[51]

Shirley, Charlotte's second published novel, was not the great success *Jane Eyre* had been, but its favorable reception established Charlotte's fame. London literary society had been intrigued by the mystery surrounding the authorship of *Jane Eyre*, and that interest had been heightened by Charlotte's dedication of the second edition to William Makepeace Thackeray—whose work she admired—for the plot of *Jane Eyre* bore a slight but unfortunate resemblance to certain facts of Thackeray's life. Speculation concerning the identity of Currer Bell ran high, and when the local color of *Shirley* led to discovery of "his" true identity, literary London was eager to meet the middle-aged spinster from a Yorkshire parsonage whose descriptions of burning passion rang so surprisingly true.

Charlotte did not enjoy the attempts to lionize her: ill, depressed, and painfully shy by nature, she was often tongue-tied in the social gatherings which honored her. Yet the stimulation of these activities at least offered a change from bleak and lonely Haworth, where every object, every scene, brought to mind her lost sisters. Determined to face and accept the fact that her life was and seemed likely to continue to be filled with pain, she strove to take what pleasure she could from the new acquaintances and friendships that her literary fame brought her, but she also stoically cautioned herself not to become too dependent on what she feared were at best transitory and shallow relationships.

Writing to Ellen Nussey from London, she remarked, "You seem to think me in such a happy, enviable position; pleasant moments I have, but it is usually a pleasure I am obliged to repel and check, which cannot benefit the future, but only add to its solitude, which is no more to be relied on than the sunshine of one summer's day. I pass portions of many a night in extreme sadness."[52] Thus she tempered every pleasure with the realistic but depressing awareness that even minor delights were fleeting and dependent upon a reputation she might find it impossible to maintain. She longed to begin another novel to prove herself worthy of her new friends' interest, to satisfy her publisher's expectations, and to escape through imagination from the despair which constantly threatened her.

For George Smith, the head of the publishing firm, and for William Smith Williams and James Taylor, his employees—all of whom had treated her with great personal kindness—Charlotte felt real affection; and she worried and felt guilty that she could not immediately produce another book and so fulfill her obligation. Yet in her letters of 1850 and 1851, she sadly reported again and again that low spirits and poor health kept her from making any real progress on a new novel. Never able to write when uninspired, she was during this period when she fruitlessly willed herself to work, unwittingly collecting the material which she would weld together with Angrian elements and with her memories of her Brussels experience to form her greatest and last novel, *Villette*.

Even when she was finally able to begin serious work on it, she found the writing of *Villette* painful in the extreme: never before had she begun a novel without the sympathetic counsel of minds attuned to her own. From childhood, the Brontës had written for one another; and when the sisters had begun their professional careers, though all maintained great independent critical judgment, they continued the practice of constantly consulting one another by gathering together every evening to read aloud what each had written alone during the day. Charlotte had written *The Professor* and *Jane Eyre* while Emily and Anne were well; she had begun *Shirley* when all were feeling the first joy of success; but Charlotte now wrote utterly alone—and her lonely agony became the theme of the book she drove herself to finish.

While working on *Villette*, she wrote to Ellen, "my life is a pale blank and often a very weary burden—and . . . the future sometimes appals me. . . . The evils that now and then wring a groan from my heart—lie in position—not that I am a *single* woman and likely to remain a *single* woman—but because I am a *lonely* woman and likely to be *lonely*. But it cannot be helped and therefore *imperatively must be borne*—and borne too with as few words about it as may be."[53] The same stoicism with which she viewed her own life she brought to a critical analysis of her current heroine, some of whose experiences so closely parallel her own. Writing to her publisher, to whom she had already sent the first two volumes of *Vil-*

lette, she said: "I consider that [Lucy Snowe] *is* both morbid and weak at times; her character sets up no pretensions to unmixed strength, and anybody living her life would necessarily become morbid."[54] Completed in November, 1852, *Villette* faithfully reflects the state of Charlotte's mind as she wrote it; as Harriet Martineau noted in her review of the book, "An atmosphere of pain hangs about the whole. . . ."[55]

Charlotte's long task was over and well over; *Villette* was enthusiastically received, but its success did not bring her happiness. In her personal life nothing had changed except for the worse: her aging father made greater demands upon her for companionship; her friendly relationship with her publisher had been permanently harmed by her last novel, which she had written partly to fulfill her professional obligation to him. Dr. John Bretton and his mother—major characters in *Villette*—were clearly based on George Smith and his mother; and although Mr. Smith had urged her to alter the third volume, she had refused to do so. The members of the firm were still courteous and kind, but the old affectionate bond between Charlotte and Smith, Elder and Company, which had helped sustain her after her sisters' death, was weakening. In the spring of 1854—a year after *Villette* was published, Charlotte wrote to George Smith with her usual stoicism, saying, "In the course of the year that is gone, Cornhill and London have receded a long way from me; the links of communication have waxed very frail and few. It must be so in this world. All things considered, I don't wish it otherwise."[56]

V   *Marriage and Death*

The year of 1853 and the spring of 1854 had brought Charlotte a new problem: shortly after finishing *Villette*, she was surprised and dismayed to receive a proposal of marriage from her father's curate, Arthur Bell Nicholls. Confronted by her father's furious rage, which led Charlotte to return an immediate and "distinct refusal,"[57] Nicholls handed in his resignation and prepared to depart; and Charlotte, although she insisted she did not love him, found his obvious suffering hard to bear, because it was, indirectly, caused by herself. He begged her to at least accept and answer his letters; and although she was a dutiful daughter, her compassionate nature and her knowledge of what it was to feel unrequited love made her agree to this plan. Thus Charlotte thrust herself into an impossible situation: caught between a heartbroken lover and an angry father, she was, as she said to Ellen Nussey, *"entirely passive. I may be losing the purest gem, and to me far the most precious life can give—genuine attachment—or I may be escaping the yoke of a morose temper. In this doubt conscience will not suffer me to take one step in opposition to papa's will. . . . So I just leave the matter where we must leave all important matters."*[58]

Her unwillingness to act was in part the result of her weary disappointment with life. A highly passionate woman whose imaginative fantasies always focused on romantic love, Charlotte was unwilling to compromise. To settle for a marriage which offered only financial and social security was to her odious, and for this reason she had refused the proposals of three other men. At twenty-three, when she seemed doomed to the drudgery of teaching, she had rejected the eligible Henry Nussey, Ellen's brother, on the grounds that, "though I esteemed, though I had a kindly leaning towards him, because he is an amiable and well-disposed man, yet I had not, and could not have, that intense attachment which would make me willing to die for him; and if ever I marry, it must be in that light of adoration that I will regard my husband."[59] In Brussels, she had found such a man in the already married M. Heger; and this experience had left her more than ever aware of the difference between passion and friendly affection. For Nicholls, she at first felt not even much liking—only pity; yet as he continued to write to her, her opposition to his suit weakened. Whatever the exact history of their courtship—whether she was flattered by his perseverance, worn out by his appeals, or moved by his hopeless suffering in which she saw the image of what her own had been—in the spring of 1854, she accepted him.

She was married on June 29, 1854; and her letters to Ellen during the next months chronicle the progress of her feeling for her husband, indicating that as he became her "dear boy,"[60] she did achieve at least a small share of happiness from the relationship. Her life became filled more than ever with domestic duties. Mr. Brontë had agreed that Nicholls should resume his curacy at Haworth, and Charlotte now kept house for and peace between the two antagonistic and possessive men who loved her. Having little time and, perhaps, less need for the compulsive fantasies out of which her fiction was created, she continued to write only a little, beginning several drafts of a novel which makes use of Angrian situations and characters.[61]

But whatever contentment she found in marriage was brief. On a November walk with her husband to see a waterfall on the moors, she caught a cold which, complicated by the early stages of pregnancy, brought about a physical decline. During the weeks of illness which followed, she bravely insisted to her sorrowing husband and father that she was improving; and on hearing Nicholl's prayer for her recovery, she remarked in protest or surprise, "Oh! I am not going to die, am I? He will not separate us, we have been so happy."[62] But on Easter eve, March 31, 1855, less than a month before her thirty-ninth birthday, Charlotte Brontë was dead.

CHAPTER 2

Early Unpublished Writings

WHEN Charlotte Brontë wrote in the preface to *The Professor* that this first novel was the product of a "pen . . . worn a good deal in a practice of some years," she was referring to a long literary apprenticeship spent compulsively chronicling the events which occurred in her imaginary "infernal world." This early material—written between 1829 and 1839, and comprising hundreds of thousands of words—richly deserves attention, since it not only illuminates Charlotte's adult novels but also offers a unique opportunity to examine a great novelist's technical development and the means by which she remodels private fantasies to suit the demands of her conscience and her public.

A study of the juvenilia is no easy task, for the individual manuscripts are the component parts of a complex saga which describes in particular detail the political and social history of the imaginary West African kingdom of Angria and the Glasstown Confederacy of which Angria is a part. During her ten-year apprenticeship, Charlotte obsessively returned again and again to this subject; instead of abandoning old characters, settings, and situations for new ones, she chose to revise, refine, and retell her story. The intensity of her fascination is made clear in her descriptions of the creative process which produced Glasstown and Angria: the world she wrote about seemed to her to have an independent existence; it possessed her so completely that she frequently closed her eyes and allowed her pen to move automatically over the page. Thus she speaks not of *inventing* these realms, but of being lifted by vision to see and hear what is happening in another world:

Never shall I, Charlotte Brontë, forget what a voice of wild and wailing music now came thrillingly to my mind's—almost to my body's—ear; nor how distinctly I, sitting in the schoolroom at Roe-head, saw the Duke of

Zamorna leaning against that obelisk, with the mute marble Victory above him, the fern waving at his feet, his black horse turned loose grazing among the heather, the moonlight so mild and so exquisitely tranquil, sleeping upon that vast and vacant road, and the African sky quivering and shaking with stars expanded above all. I was quite gone. I had really utterly forgot where I was and all the gloom and cheerlessness of my situation.[1]

Unable and, in part, unwilling to free herself from her visionary world, Charlotte tried as she grew older to remodel its details in conformity with insights afforded by her increasing aesthetic and psychological maturity. As she sought to explain the motives which underlay actions she had so vividly imagined in the past, she continually reexamined key incidents in the plot and elaborated upon their cause and consequence. The resulting Byzantine complexities of the juvenilia make it necessary to summarize the major stages in the development of the plot and the relationships of the major characters before attempting a critical commentary.

I Actors, Setting, and Plot

For several years before the Brontë children began to record their fantasies in writing, they created tales about the activities of Branwell's wooden soldiers, to whom they had assigned names and personalities. Each child became the protector of one special soldier: Emily and Anne chose for their particular attention Parry and Ross, named for the Arctic explorers William Edward Parry and John Ross; Branwell, whose original choice had been Bonaparte, renamed his hero Sneaky; Charlotte chose as her special favorite the Duke of Wellington. The story which gradually evolved took the "Young Men," as the soldiers were collectively known, to the West Coast of Africa. Here, with the help of despotic Genii (the children themselves), the Young Men defeated the aboriginal inhabitants in a fierce war and established the Glasstown Confederacy made up of four provinces—Parrysland, Rossesland, Sneakysland, and Wellingtonsland. In 1829, inspired by his love of *Blackwood's*, a popular magazine, Branwell began writing tiny booklets containing articles and poems chronicling the activities of the soldiers. Charlotte was his eager collaborator, and from 1829 until 1831, when she was sent away to Roe Head School, she also wrote accounts of the establishment and development of the Glasstown Confederacy under the rule of her particular hero, the Duke of Wellington, and his two sons, Arthur (also known as Lord Douro) and Charles Wellesley. A main source of the drama in the early materials derives from these three essentially virtuous characters' conflict with Branwell's new hero, Rogue, a proto-Byronic villain. While at school, Charlotte had little time to write, but during vacation periods, she contributed to the story, which during her absence, Branwell both expanded and particularized with new details of past and present political and military history. Meanwhile, Emily and Anne abandoned Glasstown and established Gondal, their own fantasy kingdom.

Her education at Roe Head completed, Charlotte returned home in 1832 and began anew to collaborate with Branwell on the Glasstown saga, which underwent a major transformation as the result of new events in both the political and domestic spheres. Arthur Wellesley, Lord Douro, gradually usurped his father's dominant position in Charlotte's writing; and as he gained importance, Charlotte altered his character, adding more and more Byronic qualities, chief among which were a magnetic power over and a cavalier attitude toward women. In earlier sketches, Charlotte described Douro's romantic love for a sweet, passive young girl, Marian Hume, whom he eventually married and who bore him a son; but in 1833, both Charlotte and Branwell moved their focus to Douro's relationship with a new heroine, Mary Percy—daughter of Rogue, now known as Alexander Percy.

Douro and Mary love passionately at first sight; and Marian, knowing she is powerless to command her husband's fidelity, dies of a broken heart. Douro, having given his infant son into the keeping of his mistress Mina Laury, marries Mary, whom he soon begins to torture with hints of his marital infidelity. As Douro's private life undergoes these dramatic changes, his public role is also transformed; after blocking Napoleon's invasion of the land east of the Glasstown Confederacy, Douro demands through Percy, now his ally, that parliament grant him sovereignty over the area he defended. When his demand is met, a new kingdom called Angria— comprised of the provinces of Etrei, Calabar, Douro, Arundel, Northangerland, Zamorna, and Angria—is formed under the control of Douro, who receives the titles of Duke of Zamorna and Emperor Adrian of Angria.

Douro, now commonly referred to as Zamorna, and his wife Mary soon fall prey to the machinations of her father, Percy. Although Zamorna has rewarded his father-in-law with the title of Earl of

Northangerland and with the position of prime minister, Percy is dissatisfied; and motivated by ambition and jealousy, he creates trouble for Zamorna in the Angrian parliament and among the citizenry. The manuscripts of 1834 and 1836 describe the outbreak and progress of a long war in which Zamorna struggles to maintain control of a kingdom that is threatened by internal rebellion and by invasion.

Although Charlotte began her three-year career as a teacher at Miss Wooler's School in the summer of 1835, during school holidays she eagerly returned to the Angrian saga and contributed a series of writings which concentrated on the psychological effect of the rebellion on Zamorna, Mary, Percy, and Mina Laury. In accounts written in 1837, the final phase of Angria's history begins when Zamorna triumphs over his foes and reinstates Mary as his queen after having earlier abandoned her as a means of revenging himself upon his father-in-law. Charlotte's last Angrian manuscripts deal with Zamorna's increasingly complex affairs of the heart and focus primarily on his relationships with two of his mistresses, Mina Laury and Caroline Vernon, and with his bitterly jealous wife, Mary.

II *Guilt and Growing Mastery*

At the age of twenty-three, Charlotte consciously severed relations with this fictional world, because she had come to feel that the mental activity which produced it was dangerously seductive; but ironically, in rejecting Angrian characters and history, she cast out only that material which had come to limit rather than to facilitate her exploration of the themes of passion thwarted and unleashed, violence, and threatened identity which are the essential core of her imaginative vision. During the ten years she wrote about her "world below," her emotions, insights, and understanding matured; but the heroes and heroines of her adult novels, like those she wrote about in childhood, are always the victims of their own violent emotions and of others' unpredictable malevolence.

The childish ingenuity—even crudity—of the literary devices to which Charlotte resorted as a young author may have served to focus her attention on and to sustain her interest in violence and passion. For example, recourse to the simple explanation "magic was at work" enabled her to dismiss the laws of causality and to explore with unrestrained relish incidents which, without supernatural intervention, would result in an early termination of the saga. Since the Genii who ruled the destinies of all could resurrect a hero or a villain, Charlotte could safely revel in the treacherous murder of her hero, in the murderer's cynical refusal to repent, and in his horrible punishment of death by torture.[2] Magic also permitted a tentative, safe exploration of subjects too advanced, complex, or even distasteful for realistic treatment by a young, ambitious author. Attracted to the theme of sexual passion, jealousy, and betrayal in even her earliest writing, Charlotte employs supernatural intervention to avoid difficult material, as in "The Fairy Gift" (1830), in which a sprite rescues the hero from his insane wife's sexual jealousy, or as in "The Bridal" (1832), in which the Byronic hero's marital infidelity is excused on the grounds that his mistress used magic to lure the passionate man away from his wife.

But it must be stressed that Charlotte avoided such material only because it was for the moment beyond her literary powers, not because of her inhibitions: early and late, the most striking quality of her fictional world is its violence. In the adult novels, characters smolder with rage and desire which only occasionally breaks out into physical action but which consistently drives them to brutalize others psychologically. In Glasstown and Angria, physical restraint is unknown; and the basic plot line focuses on war, rebellion, political chaos, and family disintegration. The central incident in the earliest narration is the destruction of the aboriginal Ashantee tribe after "many bloody and obstinate battles" which reduce the land to "the wildest and most appalling desolation which the mind of man can conceive of."[3]

Once in control of the disputed territory, the English colonists—men who consider cruelty and pride to be the requisites of power and the hallmarks of nobility—establish a strife-torn society. The very descriptions of the Angrian leaders suggest their proud, tempestuous natures. Charlotte's first hero, the great Duke of Wellington, whose "appearance came up to [the] highest notions of what a great General ought to be," has a "stern forehead, noble Roman nose, compressed disdainful lip" and "a certain expression of sarcasm about his mouth which showed that he considered many of those with whom he associated much beneath him" (*MUW*, I, 37). Percy has a "polished" manner, but "his mind is deceitful, bloody, and cruel" (*MUW*, I, 42). Lord Douro, originally "mild and humane but very courageous, grateful for any favour that is done, and ready to forgive injuries" (*MUW*, I, 38), becomes the Byronic Zamorna, a "keen, glorious being," whose "glancing" eyes "bode no good": "Man nor woman could ever gather more than a troubled, fitful happiness from their kindest light. Satan gave them their glory to deepen the midnight gloom that always follows where their lustre has fallen most lovingly" (*MUW*, I, 361).

These vicious, proud men control not so much a society as a mob of ruthless individualists who, bound together only by proximity, feel no need to inhibit their fierce passions. In such a world, the common forms of courtesy are disregarded; in fact, as a matter of course, the winner of a debate is "challenged . . . to single combat" (*MUW*, I, 58); a man who marries above his station is openly "despised" by his guests and "insulted . . . with impunity" by his servants (*MUW*, I, 55). The common folk of the city witness impassively as two of "some 20 or 30 naked, lean, miserable-looking children" are cast into a "fiery brazier" where they "fling themselves into all imaginable attitudes, till their extremities [are] entirely consumed" (*MUW*, I, 229–30).

The family unit is torn by the same violence which rends the fabric of city and state; for brother turns against brother; and parents, children, husbands, and wives battle murderously. The Wellesley brothers are filled with such hatred for one another that Charles tells a vicious story about his brother's faithlessness "out of malignity for the injuries that have lately been done me";[4] and in another tale, his brother, Douro, savagely beats Charles and then threatens to "hardly leave a strip of skin on his carcass" if he offends again (*LA*, 7). In "The Fairy Gift," a witch-wife rushes upon her husband, who has discovered her magic rites, and attempts to strangle him (*MUW*, I, 56). Maddened by jealousy, Percy turns on his wife, saying, "You shall not die the easy death of having your brains blown out. No! I'll thrust this sharp blade slowly through you, that you may feel and enjoy the torture" (*MUW*, I, 260).

As Charlotte passed from childhood and adolescence to maturity, her increased experience, perception, and technical ability modify the Angrian world. Verisimilitude takes precedence over the fantastic. Perhaps the most obvious indication of the increasing realism of her work appears in late stories such as "Mina Laury" (1838) and "Caroline Vernon" (1839), in which the nominally African landscape comes to resemble that of northern England and Yorkshire: "The air is dimmed with snow careering through it in wild whirls—the sky is one mass of congealed tempest—heavy, wan, & icy—the trees rustle their frozen branches against each other in a blast bitter enough to flay alive the flesh that should be exposed to its sweep."[5] Yorkshire dialect, attitudes, and concerns also intrude. A bluff, blunt military man dismisses his wife's terrifying dreams in accents which recall Joseph's speech in *Wuthering Heights* (*MUW*, II, 384), and another character pokes cynical fun at the assumed piety of his landlord and the activities of Methodist Ranters in a scene set not in the never-never land of Angria but in mid-nineteenth-century Yorkshire (*MUW*, II, 281–82).

Deriving great satisfaction from realistic portrayal, Charlotte worked consciously to remodel her fictional world. In 1836 she invokes her muse to "paint to the life," "detail with graphic skill," "scribe so well that each separate voice shall speak out of the page in changeful tone," and "shew us even those details that give truest life to the picture," for all these characteristics have the power to "astonish us" (*MUW*, II, 125). Charlotte's invocation is highly significant, for it reveals her changed attitude toward her materials, a change dictated by growing awareness of a new sort of involvement in the writer's craft. Later in the same year, Charlotte describes the pleasure given her by one of Branwell's Angrian accounts, and her delight derives not from entering vicariously into represented dramatic action but from feeding her imagination on scenes carefully and realistically delineated in minute detail:

About a week since I got a letter from Branwell containing a most exquisitely characteristic [Angrian] epistle. . . . I lived on its contents for days; in every pause of employment it came chiming in like some sweet bar of music—bringing with it agreeable thoughts such as I had for many weeks been a stranger to—some representing scenes such as might arise in consequence of that unexpected letter, some unconnected with it, referring to other events, another set of feelings. These were not striking and stirring scenes of incident—no—they were tranquil and retired in their character, such as might every day be witnessed in the inmost circles of highest society. A curtain seemed to rise and discover to me the Duchess as she might appear when newly risen and lightly dressed for the morning— discovering her father's letter in the contents of the mail which lies on her breakfast-table. There seems nothing in such an idea as that, but the localities of the picture were so graphic, the room so distinct, the clear fire of morning, the window looking upon no object but a cold October sky, except when you draw very near and look down on a terrace far beneath, and, at a still dizzier distance, on a green court with a fountain and rows of stately limes—beyond, a wide road and wider river, and a vast metropolis. (*MUW*, II, 256–57)

The pleasure Charlotte received from the imaginative contemplation and creation of scenes realistically portrayed marks the last accounts of her fantasy world. In "Caroline Vernon," Wellesley House, the home of the ruler of Angria, retains its grand title but shrinks to a suburban villa. The Duke and Duchess of Zamorna shed the garments of romance to become a blustering, guilty husband and a foolish, protective wife. Mary, whose tortured love for her erring Zamorna was once the most interesting and pathetic of subjects to Charlotte, becomes an unperceptive, jealous, doting housewife waiting up to interrogate a husband guilty of keeping late hours; Zamorna, her husband, once described as a figure of "faultless elegance" with "features . . . regularly beautiful" (*MUW*, I, 241), is shown "stepp[ing] on his toes like a magnified dancing-master." He who once drew all women to him with a glance, now creeps into his darkened house like "a large Tom-Cat" (*FN*, 331).

Charlotte's handling of the romantic dreams of Caroline Vernon, her last Angrian heroine, indicates clearly that the maturing artist has not only viewed her past imaginative ventures with detached amusement but has also realized the literary potential of objective—even ironic—introspection and description; for what she here presents as being ridiculous fantasy actually parodies many passages in her earlier writings:

. . . something there was of a Hero—yet a nameless, a formless, a mystic being—a dread shadow—that crowded upon Miss Vernon's soul—haunted her day & night when she had nothing useful to occupy her head or her hands—I almost think she gave him the name of Ferdinand Alonzo Fitz-Adolphus, but I don't know—the fact was he frequently changed his designation—being sometimes no more than simple Charles Seymour or Edward Clifford, & at other times soaring to the titles of Harold, Aurelius Rinaldo, Duke of Montmorency di Valdacella—a very fine man no doubt—though whether he was to have golden or raven hair or straight or acquiline proboscis she had not quite decided—however, he was to drive all before him in the way of fighting—to conquer the world & build himself a city like Babylon—only it was to be in the moorish style—& there was to be a palace called the Alhambra—where Mr Harold Aurelius was to live, taking upon himself the title of Caliph, & she, Miss C. Vernon, the professor of Republi-

can principles, was to be his chief Lady & to be called the Sultana Zara-
Esmerelda—with at least a hundred slaves to do her bidding—as for the
gardens of roses & the Halls of Marble & the diamonds & fine pearls & the
rubies—it would be vanity to attempt a description of such heavenly
sights—the reader must task his imagination & try if he can conceive them.
(*FN*, 312–13) ·

Charlotte's growing interest in realism and her increasing perception and technical skill lead her to probe the complexity of character. The idea that appearances belie reality, hinted at in the earliest
pieces by figures who are witches and magicians in disguise, becomes a dominant concern in later works and leads to her analysis of
the complex emotional states that play a role in an involved response
to life. After Zamorna's defeat by the Angrian rebels and his subsequent exile, Charlotte turns her attention in "The Return of
Zamorna" (1836–1837) to the reaction of his deserted wife, Mary
Henrietta. Although Charlotte follows the convention of the day by
describing her grief-stricken heroine's fall into a physical decline,
the ambitious young author does not rest content with convention;
rather, she probes deeply into Mary's emotional state, matching
psychological insight with impressive literary technique. When
Mary rises "wan and pallid from the bed that a month since it
seemed she would never leave again," she enters a terrible existence: her body lives, but her soul has died. Unable to bear the
memory of the past she has lost, she is unable to accept the present
to which it has led; thus, her identity is stripped from her, for to call
herself either mother or wife is to remind herself of happiness that is
forever gone. The stirring of memories she is desperate to repress is
suggested both by her question "was I ever married?" and by the
fact that although she "continued to wear round her neck, a little
miniature of the Duke . . . she never opened the case that con-
tained it."

Fearing to unlock the past, she walks in a trance through the maze
of corridors in her winter-besieged palace. Her spiritual deadness is
objectified in falling leaves and autumnal groves, symbols of sterility
and death, and the aimless wandering of her body through endless,
echoing passages suggests the confused straying of her mind
through the labyrinth of past experience: "The last days of Autumn
were now dimly closing. . . . the leaf-strewn walks and embrowned
groves of Alnwick prophesied how nigh were the snows of Winter. . . . Too feeble to bear the chill . . . , she never walked but in

the lengthened and sounding corridors . . . and there all day long
the light rustle of her dress might be heard as she traversed the
measured walk with noiseless and languid tread, more like a flitting
shade than a living woman" (*MUW*, II, 285–87).

There is yet another level of significance in Charlotte's description. As Angria's queen drifts through a decaying world, her war-
torn nation sinks toward death. The impression of destruction which
permeates the entire passage culminates in the image of the
pearl-like tear which falls from Mary's eye. Consistently described as
ornamented with "chains" and rings of pearl, Mary is herself "a
priceless pearl which a strong man had found and which he kept and
guarded jealously" (*MUW*, II, 27); now the strong man is gone; the
rich setting of Zamorna Palace, with its "warm lights" and "rich
deep sombre hangings" (*MUW*, II, 26), has been ravaged. And the
tear on Mary's eyelid, which falls "like a single pearl on the pavement" (*MUW*, II, 286), is symbolic of Mary herself, the most trea-
sured, the most guarded jewel of the kingdom. The destruction is
complete: physically and mentally, Mary dies; and her land and her
world die with her.

III *Percy and Zamorna*

The impulse toward self-destruction which is implicit in this description of Mary's responses continued to intrigue Charlotte and
ultimately became the focus of her juvenile writings. As her growing
insights and technical ability enabled her to provide more complex
character sketches of the individuals engaged in the never-ending
series of battles upon which Branwell insisted, she began to use the
framework of war to probe into the problem of psychic conflict; for
she saw political strife as emblematic of and stemming from ambivalent and mutually destructive internal impulses. The very fact that
the two men who most actively attempt to overthrow Emperor
Zamorna are bound to him by familial and quasi-familial ties intensified her perception that actual and potential warfare is symbolic of
the tearing apart of what is by nature a single unit: Quashia, who
threatens to invade Angria and to drive out the English colonists,
was raised as Zamorna's foster brother; Percy, who foments internal
rebellion, is Zamorna's surrogate father, father-in-law, prime minister, and spiritual twin.

The relationship between Percy and Zamorna—which was from
the beginning the crucial source of conflict in the overall plot of the

saga—increasingly tantalized Charlotte as she strove to provide psychological motivation for the actions she and Branwell in their earliest writings had attributed to these two central figures. Again and again she returns to the intriguing riddle of the bond that unites the two in mutual ruin; and her awareness of her fascination with this topic is apparent when, at one point, after having once again recapitulated the history of the Zamorna-Percy relationship, she remarks: "All this I have written before, but the subject is a strange one and will bear recurring to, and the fact is, when I once get upon the topic . . . I cannot help running on in the old track at a most unconscionable rate" (*MUW*, II, 361).

Gradually, Charlotte perceives and clarifies a meaningful pattern in the interaction between these two men, Percy and Zamorna. Drawing upon Grecian and Christian tradition, using ideas gleaned from Shakespeare, Milton, and Byron, Charlotte finally interprets the political battle between Zamorna and Percy as the epic struggle of beings bound together by a mutual love and hate for each other and for themselves. In one of her last Angrian pieces, "The Duke of Zamorna" (1838), she attempts to bring together the pieces of the psychological puzzle. Four years earlier, in "The Wool is Rising," Branwell had explained that Percy, fearing his young sons had inherited his own evil nature, condemned them to death.[6] Making use of this information to illuminate the background of the confederacy between Percy and Zamorna, Charlotte now describes how Percy, "spent almost with sin" after the infanticide, chose young Douro as his "confidant" and revealed to him "the tenderest, the holiest feeling his heart had ever known."

Although, we are told, if Percy "had discerned anything like attachment to his person in any other man or boy," he would have responded with "intense and eternal hate," he accepted Douro's "glances of feeling—clashing, ardent, enthusiastic" (*MUW*, II, 360). Too proud to serve another, Percy finds his love for Douro doubly intolerable, for it forces awareness of his emotional dependency upon him while winning him the subordinate position of prime minister in Zamorna's Angrian government. Thus Charlotte is able to support and clarify her previous assertion in "The History of Angria III" (1836) that Percy's rebellious acts, inexplicable in pragmatic terms, are indeed "not a disease in themselves, but merely the symptoms of some grand latent malady" (*MUW*, II, 139) in Percy's heart and soul.

Her analysis of Zamorna's motivation is much more complete. Always the central figure in Charlotte's Angrian writings, Zamorna is transformed from a Prince Charming, a child of good fortune, into a tortured and doomed man. Possessing a personal magnetism that gives him virtually total political and sexual power, Zamorna is driven by inner defects to destroy those he loves, his empire, and ultimately himself. Much of Charlotte's later Angrian material is devoted to an analysis of his complex character. In "The History of Angria III," Charlotte remarks that "notwithstanding [Zamorna's] outside shew of rich vigorous health, . . . in the timber of this stately tree there was a flaw which would eat ere the lapse of many years to its heart" (*MUW*, II, 155). The flaw is his dependency upon Percy, who has betrayed him, but whom he continues against his will to love and to whom he believes his fate is linked by destiny. Conceiving of himself and Percy as two halves of a whole which seeks a dissolution that will bring ruin on itself and all about it, Zamorna says of his antagonist, "You are a fiend . . . I'm no better, and we two united / Each other's happiness have fiend-like blighted" (*MUW*, II, 240).

In Charlotte's writings, the civil war Percy instigates against Zamorna thus emblematizes and expresses the love-hate struggle of two men whose self-destructive rage encompasses the nation which they created together and which, therefore, represents to each a mutually hated interdependence. In "The History of Angria III," Zamorna's supporters rightfully accuse him of seeking not so much military victory as private revenge; and Zamorna, although he remains adamant in his purpose, acknowledges the truth of this interpretation. Turning to his Home Secretary, General Warner, Zamorna announces,

two living creatures in the world know the nature of the relations that have existed between Alexander Percy and myself. From the very beginning in my inmost soul, . . . I swore that if he broke those bonds and so turned to vanity and scattered in the air sacrifices that I had made and words that I had spoken; if he made as dust and nothingness causes for which I have endured jealousies and burning strife and emulations amongst those I loved; if he froze feelings that in me are like living fire, I would have revenge. (*MUW*, II, 156)

The relationship Zamorna here discusses is explained further in "The Duke of Zamorna," written two years later. Charlotte recounts how Zamorna had once sought [Percy's] society—followed his footsteps—hung spellbound on his persuasive lips—insinuated his way to his confidence— . . . and Douro was not repulsed: he was retained—almost clung to.

True [Percy] broke upon his young comrade sometimes with fury, and at other times he seemed to freeze and turn away with hollow coldness from his enthusiasm. This [Douro] felt at his heart's core. (*MUW*, II, 360)

Zamorna, therefore, sees Percy's overt political rebellion primarily as the last and most drastic of a series of emotional withdrawals and rejections. And his thwarted love for Percy drives him to seek military triumph over him as a means of gaining personal revenge and of proving his psychological dominance; but he foreknows that victory over Percy will be final defeat for himself, as he admits when he cries out in anguish and rage, "He has no heart and I'll rend mine from my bosom before its quick hot pulsations shall interfere with what I see, with what I feel, with what I anticipate by day and night. Why else were we born in one century? His sun should have set before mine rose, if their blended shining was not destined to set Earth on fire" (*MUW*, II, 30). Thus for Zamorna the political and military struggle against Percy is, in fact, the acting out of a death-wish, a suicide, the "tearing up [of] something whose roots had taken deep hold in [his] very heart of hearts" (*FN*, 137). He acknowledges that his battle with Percy produces a "mental anguish" which "shortens . . . my very brief allotment of life on earth. . . . I loved Percy, and what it is costing me to send him to the D—1!!" (*MUW*, II, 158).

So uncontrollable is Zamorna's desire for omnipotence that he would rather destroy the thing he loves than be thwarted in his desire to possess it totally: Angria, the nation he lovingly created; Mary, his adored wife; Percy, his beloved surrogate father—all become the targets of his hate and are destroyed by him in a series of actions which only increase his agony. By thus using the civil war that he wages with monomaniac fury as the expression of Zamorna's sadomasochistic tendencies, Charlotte establishes the link between sexual desire and the willingness to inflict and suffer pain which informs all her work. That she equates Zamorna's emperorship with aggressive sexual potency is apparent in his address to the kingdom he has willfully "ruined," for he remembers his days of political power as the time when

> I was king in thee,
> And when thy wildest mountains, heather palled,
> With all their iron vassalage knew me,

And my land's daughters, now with bondage galled,
Were as the Gordon red deer, chainless, free,
And thousands of their ruby lips have known
The touch of [Zamorna's] when he claims his own.
                                              (*MUW*, II, 246)

Angria had once been "gilded by [his] hand from the crown of [her]
head to the sole of [her] foot," but she has been betrayed by her
lover-king, who "should have been [her] mantle and . . . shield,"
her "warder, [her] counsellor." The effect of his "rashness
. . . cruelty, [and] selfishness" (*MUW*, II, 162–63) is, significantly
enough, presented as the symbolic rape of his queen, Mary, who is
both an emblem of his nation and his deserted wife. Left free to
invade the capital Zamorna has abandoned, Quashia, the savage
aboriginal heir to the land, marches through the "defiled and vio-
lated" city, and at last enters into the undefended private rooms of
the palace, where he lolls "intoxicated to ferocious insensibility"
upon the couch of the Queen he has long desired:

Aye, where she had lain imperially robed and decked with pearls, every
waft of her garments as she moved diffusing perfume, her beauty slumber-
ing and still glowing as dreams of [Zamorna] for whom she kept herself in
such hallowed and shrine-like separation wandered over her soul, on her
own silken couch [stretched] a swart and sinewy Moor. . . . I knew it to be
Quashia himself, and well could I guess why he had chosen the Queen of
Angria's sanctuary for the scene of his solitary revelling. . . . he was full
before my eyes, lying in his black dress on the disordered couch, his sable
hair dishevelled on his forehead, his tusk-like teeth gleaming vindictively
through his parted lips, his brown complexion flushed with wine, and his
broad chest heaving wildly as the breath issued in snorts from his distended
nostrils.[7]

From 1836 to 1838 most of Charlotte's writings concern Zamorna's decision to make Mary suffer, even die, to achieve what he
knows will be a Pyrrhic victory over Percy; and this concern leads
Charlotte to probe ever more deeply into psychological complexities
and to examine more fully her controlling theme of the destructive
power of sexual desire. At one point, Mary says that Zamorna sees
her as "the bodiless link between himself and my terrible father"
(*MUW*, II, 147) whom Zamorna had "loved intensely" (*MUW*, II,
330) but who had defied his will and betrayed his love. Mary is the

perfect victim not only because of the effect her agony and death will have upon her father but also because she is the incarnation of Percy in feminine form and thus, unlike her father, is susceptible to Zamorna's sexual charm:

> [Mary's] sweet eyes
> Showed in their varied lustre—changing, fleeing—
> Such warm and intense passion—that which lies
> In [Percy's] own breast and, save to the All-seeing,
> Not fully known to any, could not rise
> To stronger inspiration than their ray
> Revealed when I had waked her nature's wildest play.
>
> (*MUW*, II, 241)

These lines provide the key to the situation. Percy remains forever the enigma; the passions which govern him are fully divined only by the "All-seeing"; but Zamorna, by virtue of his sexual power, controls Mary totally: it is he who "waked her nature's wildest play." Unlike her father, she does not reject Zamorna's passion; instead, she delights in it, pleads for it, and will die without it:

> "Why have you chained me to you, [Zamorna], by
> Such days of bliss, such hours of sweet caressing,
> Such looks of glory, words of melody,
> Glimpses of all on earth that's worth possessing
> And now, when I must live with you or die
> Out of your sight distracted, every blessing
> Your hand withdraws, and, all my anguish scorning,
> You go and bid me hope for no returning?
>
> "[Zamorna], don't leave me—" then the gushing tears
> Smothered her utterance.
>
> (*MUW*, II, 328)

The equation of male potency and violence which runs throughout the Angrian writings is explicit in Zamorna's plan for victory: "In all but one quarter [Percy] is fortified and garrisoned. He can bid me [Zamorna] defiance, but one quarter [Mary] lies open to my javelin, and dipped in venom I will launch it quivering into his very spirit—so help me Hell!" (*MUW*, II, 156).

Because killing and loving are thus inextricably connected in this world, some of Charlotte's characters attempt to repress all emotion in order to avoid becoming either victims or victimizers. This response, only slightly touched upon in the Angrian writings, is fully developed in the adult novels: emotional withdrawal is chosen as a way of life by Yorke Hunsden, St. John Rivers, Mrs. Pryor, and the Reverend Helstone; it is seriously considered by Jane Eyre, Robert and Louis Moore, Lucy Snowe, Paul Emanuel, and William Crimsworth. The original of this last character is William Percy of the Angrian saga, who prides himself on having "denied [his] feelings . . . absolutely" (*MUW*, II, 390). Yet even as he thus congratulates himself, he realizes that he has imprisoned himself in a vast and empty wasteland. To him the people who crowd the thoroughfares of the capital are of no more significance than phantoms in a dream: he sees before him only a prospect of "wide Squares . . . long Streets"; and when he commands himself to "think again—surely some one breathes who will wish thee well," he admits, "I thought and thought—and all seemed vacant" (*MUW*, II, 392).

William's ability to choose an alienation so total that it is itself a kind of psychological suicide is unusual in the Angrian writings. Most of the characters in these manuscripts succumb totally and with little struggle to the passions which rage within them. Believing that human beings are by nature highly sexed, self-seeking, violent, and capable of brutality, Charlotte depicts sexual desire as an overwhelming force which robs both men and women of both the capacity and the will to defend the self against the innate aggressiveness of a lover. In the Angrian writings, all-engrossing passion blots out even the instinct for self-preservation; and the besotted individual, perceiving the sadomasochistic nature of the relationship into which he is ineluctably drawn, frequently sees death as the inevitable result, or even the equivalent of, sexual consummation. On the simplest level, the lover, therefore, offers himself willingly to the blood lust of his sexual rivals; and Lord Hartford's actions when he is spurned by Zamorna's mistress Mina Laury epitomizes this response. Knowing he can never possess her, he madly challenges Zamorna to a duel; and when a mediator attempts to intervene, saying "all is in vain, the lady in question can never be yours," Hartford answers, "I know that, Sir, & that is what makes me frantic—I have no motive left for living, & if Zamorna wants my blood, let him have it" (*FN*, 154).

In the 1836–1839 manuscripts, the focus of interest is on Zamorna's dealings with three women—Mary, Mina Laury, and Caroline Vernon; and Charlotte's treatment of these relationships suggests that men are capable of sexual response only when they subjugate and inflict pain on women and that women choose to submit themselves to sexual brutalization which leads to the loss of psychological and moral identity. Indeed, the story of Zamorna's sadistic victimization of his wife Mary, whose masochism makes her his willing accomplice, is the paradigm of sexual relationships in the early writings. In the poem "And When You Left Me" (1836), Zamorna, thinking about Mary's response to his brutality, suggests that on her own initiative she is pursuing a suicidal course: "She said she'd die for me—and now she's keeping / Her word far off at Alnwick o'er the sea" (*MUW*, II, 243).

Zamorna is quite right in his inference; for Mary, rejected by Zamorna and fearing he is dead, passively courts death by living "almost without food" and sitting "from morning to night in one place, almost in one position" (*MUW*, II, 287). Eventually, she consciously chooses death over a life of continued separation: "I adored him . . . —and Oh God, is that radiant, resistless being truly dead? Am I to feel rest for my aching agony no more? If this were my certain doom I would live not an instant longer" (*MUW*, II, 290). Returning to this theme in "Well, the Day's Toil is Over" (1837), Charlotte examines the full extent of Mary's perverse nature, suggesting that she is most fully aroused sexually when she is most threatened. Thus at the moment when Mary understands the truth and says to Zamorna, "You love me, yet you'll kill me," she feels "an electric thrill and passion [wake] / In all her veins" (*MUW*, II, 327).

IV *Mina Laury and Caroline Vernon*

In Charlotte's final Angrian stories—written between 1838 and 1839—she continued to define the sexual myth which she had been slowly evolving and which is also central to the novels of her maturity. Her last two heroines, Mina Laury and Caroline Vernon, differ greatly from each other and from Mary Percy in social position, character, and psychological maturity; but all are willing victims of the brutal male lover—Zamorna. Overwhelmed by sexual desire, they renounce social standing and brush aside moral considerations to become his slaves; and though they recognize that their relationship with him entails suffering, they find perverse pleasure in such danger and in the fear that Zamorna's aggressive sexuality awakens in them. The heroines of the adult novels are sisters of these women, all of whom are tempted to act in accordance with Shirley Keeldar's statement that in choosing a mate she "prefer[s] a *master*. . . . A man I shall find it impossible not to love, and very possible to fear."[8]

The story of Mina's relationship with Zamorna is both complex and tragic. Possessing both capacity and drive for independence, and a sensibility which makes her aware of fine moral distinctions, Mina freely chooses to sacrifice herself in order to fulfill emotional needs which she herself defines as evil because they place her in a position which she finds shameful and which robs her of worth in her own eyes. Capable of supervising the financing of Zamorna's military campaigns and the upbringing of Zamorna's son, she wins the admiration of his military supporters who, seeing her as "sagacious, clever, and earnest," "did not hesitate to communicate with her often on matters of first-rate importance" (*MUW*, II, 133).

Mina takes pleasure in her superior powers, finding a sense of herself in her ability to meet every test, as she acknowledges: "when I was at Fort Adrian and had all the yoke of governing the garrison and military household, I used to rejoice in my responsibility and feel firmer the heavier weight was assigned me to support" (*MUW*, II, 134). But her love for Zamorna vitiates these capacities: "Miss Laury belonged to the Duke of Zamorna—She was indisputably his property as much as the Lodge of Rivaux or the stately woods of Hawkscliffe, & in that light she considered herself" (*FN*, 143). Seeing herself thus, she considers herself disgraced and unworthy of contact with society. Suspicious that all must scorn her as she scorns herself ("Every body knows me . . . 'Mistress' I suppose, is branded on my brow" [*FN*, 160]), she still becomes so dependent on the man she idolizes that she says of the relationship which has corrupted her: "I've nothing else to exist for; I've no other interest in life" (*MUW*, II, 134).

Thus she is trapped in an increasingly self-destructive pattern. In "The History of Angria III," Charlotte describes how "an unconscious wish of wild intensity filled [Mina] that she were dead and buried, and insensible to the shame that overwhelmed her" (*MUW*, II, 137). And in the sketch written two years later that concludes Mina's story, her passion has led to the fatal consequence she unconsciously pursued, for she now insists, "[my] feelings [for Zamorna] . . . were so fervid . . . they effaced everything else—I lost the power of properly appreciating the value of the world's opinion, of discerning the difference between right & wrong." She is herself aware that loss of her moral sense and concomitant sacrifice of her identity add up to psychic death: "Unconnected with him my mind would be a blank—cold, dead, and susceptible only of a sense of despair" (*FN*, 147).

Charlotte Brontë's belief in the fatal power of sexual desire is nowhere more succinctly stated than in the story of this heroine. Although Mina is "strong-minded beyond her sex—active, energetic, & accomplished," her love for Zamorna makes her "weak as a child." Ultimately, "her very way of life . . . swallowed up in that of another," she comes to function merely as the extension of her vicious lover's will. That she finds pleasure in his brutalization of herself and others is made clear when Zamorna—who can respond sexually only when he has proved his total power over her by taunting her until she faints and lies "stretched at his feet"—proceeds to offer her as proof of his love, not an embrace, but the announcement that he has been willing to kill the man who threatened to take her from him. For Mina accepts his statement not only as appropriate evidence of his passion, but as the consummation of their perverse sexual relationship: "Miss Laury shuddered, but so dark & profound are the mysteries of human nature, ever allying vice with virtue, that I fear this bloody proof of her master's love brought to her heart more rapture than horror" (*FN*, 165).

"Caroline Vernon," the last of Charlotte's Angrian writings, is a study of a young girl's awakening to sexual desire, which inevitably leads her to surrender her entire identity to her lover. While the basic theme is the familiar one traced in the histories of Mary and Mina, in this sketch Charlotte examines the psychology of her heroine even more fully; by making use of interior monologue and reflective passages, she reveals the tension between fear of and desire for sexual experience. Caroline is introduced as a hoydenish fifteen-year-old girl who gives promise of great beauty and who, as the daughter of Percy and his emotionally unstable mistress Louisa Danci, has inherited a highly passionate nature and a rebellious spirit. Charlotte implies that Caroline's childish hero worship of Zamorna, who is her guardian, holds within it the seeds of sexual desire which Caroline can neither understand nor acknowledge. Her conversation with Zamorna on the eve of her departure for Paris to finish her education makes the situation plain. Zamorna, responding to her plea that he show his affection for her as openly as he had when she was a little girl, commands her to come to him; but she draws back, saying, "I don't know [why]—I didn't mean to draw back." Zamorna replies, "But you always do, Caroline, now—when I come near you—& you turn away your face from me if I kiss you, which I seldom do—because you are too old to be kissed & fondled like a child" (*FN*, 365).

In Paris, Caroline, for the first time treated as a woman, makes "discoveries concerning men & things which sometimes astounded her"; specifically, she learns that "she [is] a very attractive being & [has the power of inspiring love] in a very high degree" and that Zamorna is "a man vicious like other men—perhaps . . . more than other men—with passions that sometimes controlled him—with propensities that were often stronger than his reason—with feelings that could be reached by beauty" (*FN*, 319–23). She revaluates her love for him; but knowing he is married, she disavows any sexual interest on the grounds that such feeling would be "wicked" and insists instead that she merely wants always "to be doing something that would please him" (*FN*, 337). Yet when she is alone in the privacy of her darkened room, her passion overwhelms her moral principles: "I can't go to sleep, I'm so hot & so restless—I could bear now to see a spirit come to my bed-side and ask me what I wanted—wicked or not wicked, I would tell all—& beg it to give me the power to make the Duke of Zamorna like me better than ever he liked anybody in the world before" (*FN*, 337).

On her return from Paris, she takes "secret enjoyment . . . from the idea of shewing herself to [Zamorna]—improved as she knew she was" (*FN*, 327). And angered by her father's efforts to protect her by keeping her from Zamorna's sight, she runs off to join him, although she attempts to hide the consequences of her rash act from herself with childish fantasies: "He did not know the restless, devouring feeling she had when she thought of him . . . . she would crush the feeling & never tell that it had existed—She did not want him to love her in return—no—no—that would be wicked—She only wanted him to be kind—to think well of her, to like to have her with him—nothing more—unless indeed the Duchess of Zamorna was to happen to die, & then—" (*FN*, 349).

But when Zamorna and Caroline meet, he refuses to allow her the luxury of such equivocation; despite the fact that she has tried to present her elopement as the act of a wayward and affectionate child, she knows "he looked upon her with different eyes to what he had done, & considered her attachment to him as liable to another interpretation than the mere fondness of a Ward for her Guardian" (*FN*, 351).

Caroline is thus doomed by the mere fact that she has become sexually mature. "All the ladies in the world . . . hold the Duke of Zamorna to be matchless, irresistible" (*FN*, 315); and having become a woman, Caroline must acknowledge and act upon her all too natural desire for this man whose hypnotic sexual power both titillates and terrifies her:

Miss Vernon sat speechless—She darkly saw or rather felt the end to which all this tended, but all was fever & delirium round her—The Duke spoke again—in a single blunt & almost coarse sentence compressing what yet remained to be said. "If I were a bearded Turk, Caroline, I would take you to my Harem"—His deep voice, as he uttered this—his high-featured face, & dark large eyes, beaming bright with a spark from the depths of Gehenna, struck Caroline Vernon with a thrill of nameless dread— . . . all at once she knew him—her Guardian was gone—Something terrible sat in his place. . . . She attempted to rise—this movement produced the effect she had feared, the arm closed round her—Miss Vernon could not resist its strength, a piteous upward look was her only appeal. (*FN*, 352–53)

Thus the inevitable pattern is completed; and Caroline, like Mary and Mina, becomes the possession of Zamorna, who gloats over his sexual triumph, saying to Percy, "You cannot take her from me, & if you could—how would you prevent her return?—She would either die or come back to me now" (*FN*, 358).

"Caroline Vernon," Charlotte's last extant Angrian tale, focuses upon the moment when, having left the protective innocence of childhood behind, the heroine becomes "one of the Gleaners of Grapes in that Vineyard—where all man & woman-kind—have been plucking fruit since the world began, the Vineyard of Experience" (*FN*, 363). The quotation effectively summarizes Charlotte's view of the consequences of female sexuality. The skillful portrayal of Caroline's fluctuation between passionate ecstasy and fear foreshadows the similarly ambivalent responses of Jane Eyre, Shirley Keeldar, and Lucy Snowe to their aggressive lovers.

V *The Early Writings and the Adult Novels*

In writing the annals of Glasstown and Angria, Charlotte codified her conception of psychological truth; and despite her avowal in 1839 that she "long[ed] to quit for awhile that burning clime," the

Angrian mode of perception, synonymous as it was with her creative imagination, could not be wholly suppressed or denied. The adult novels complete the process begun years earlier of reshaping fantasy to a surface accord with reality. Not only do some of the characters from the earlier writings appear in the four novels, but Angria itself, fragmented by war and dominated by vicious and self-seeking leaders, is the paradigm of the strife-ridden Yorkshire of *Shirley*, the morally corrupt cities of *The Professor* and *Villette*, and the desolate and inimical social environment of *Jane Eyre*. Ruled by an omnipotent emperor whose acts are expressions of his destructive impulses and idiosyncratic needs, the Angrians are placed in a situation which prefigures that of the protagonists of the later works.

All of Charlotte's novels concentrate upon the individual and his own needs, rather than upon social context. The Angrian manuscripts are filled with characters who seek their private fulfillment at the expense of all others and even of society, if need be. This egoism is sometimes tempered, sometimes disguised, in the mature novels; but Charlotte's militant Protestantism in these works functions, oddly enough, to allow her heroes and heroines something of the same freedom. For by extending the basic Protestant doctrine that the individual needs no mediator between himself and God, these characters are able not only to deny the teachings of the ministers of the Church but to reject or to reinterpret Scripture in accordance with their own desires and to insist that the only true commands of God are those which conform to the individual's own deeply felt needs. This total reliance of the individual upon himself accounts for the fact that the crisis of each of Charlotte's novels comes when the protagonist reaches a crucial decision which introspection rather than the advice or teaching of others reveals to him as right.

In fact, Charlotte's assumptions about the nature of the human condition expressed in her depiction of Angria remain essentially the same in her adult novels and are in conformity with the Christian view that man is a fallen being in a fallen world. The protagonists of both her juvenile and adult fiction exist amid violence and danger. They are the prey not only of vicious enemies but also of their own passionate natures which urge them toward social and psychological destruction. And the linking of sex with self-destruction and violence which appears throughout her work echoes the fear of sexuality which is basic to Pauline doctrine.

Charlotte's own sense of her Angrian writings as dangerous and revelatory of her sinful state stems from the fact that her juvenile works imply that there is no force sufficient to control man's evil, sensual nature—and, indeed, that there is no good reason for controlling it. Glasstown and Angria are Zamorna's world: there is no power superior to his; and he, like the Byronic hero he is modeled upon, is a demonic figure. Convinced of his damnation, he ruthlessly makes others suffer, not in the hope of achieving happiness himself, but because his insatiable ego finds momentary satisfaction only in his ability to prove his power by inflicting pain. Ineluctably fascinating and, as Emperor, the holder of the reins of all social and political power, he is an omnipotent force against whom there is no defense. Those who hate him, hopeless of any remedy in law, can respond only with a viciousness similar to his own; those who love him, since they are inhabitants of a world bereft of meaningful religious, ethical, or moral standards, suffer his cruelty in an agony of self-destructive passion which they can appeal to no superior values to control.

Angria is, in a sense, the province of the id; Charlotte's superego dictated her conception of reality. The resulting tension between what she was naturally drawn to and the values she thought she should uphold is apparent in all of her adult novels. In all of these works, the unresolvable conflict between romantic fantasy and reality, passion and control, imagination and reason, is observable not only in tone but also in atmosphere and in conception of human psychology. At times the burning light of Angria flashes out, illuminating her prosaic settings and transforming them into a landscape of dream or nightmare as a ghostly nun walks the shadowy attics of a school and as a goblin laugh rings out in the third story of an English country house.

Indeed, Charlotte's struggles to subdue the subconscious self which produced Angria are echoed in the works of her maturity as again and again—and most powerfully in *Villette*—she describes the agony of the individual who discovers within himself powerful impulses, desires, and fears which are not subject to the control of the rational mind. The sexual relationships which form the center of her plots force the protagonists to recognize the claims of these latent and potentially dangerous impulses of their deeply divided natures. Priggish, smug, self-complacent, they pay lip service to the conventional values of Protestant, puritan, nineteenth-century society; but at the same time, they are highly unconventional, deeply passionate, and self-centered. Because her heroes and heroines are thus driven by antithetical desires, frustration suffuses all of Charlotte's work.

On the one hand, her central characters seek what reason tells them is desirable and attainable: position, respect, economic success, and above all, independence. But these men and women search with equal fervor for that which their romantic imaginations envision: not just for conventional love or fulfillment of burning physical passion, but for a soul mate—the one individual who meets the needs of their inner natures and who will allow them to complete themselves. For Charlotte's protagonists, no measure of social or economic success, no sense of conforming to abiding moral principles, is ever sufficient in itself—the soul mate must be sought and won. Yet because the search for and commitment to this unique human being militates against the achievement of other, more reasonable aims, no ultimate, satisfactory solution is possible. The images of abysses, sterility, fragmentation, and death which fill Charlotte Brontë's works bespeak a deep conflict within herself; and her novels reflect this tension, since they chronicle the rending internal conflict suffered by individuals who desperately desire both to be supremely independent and to be merged, twinned, with another.

CHAPTER 3

The Professor

I *The Plot*

The Professor opens with a brief summary of the events which lead twenty-year-old William Crimsworth to seek employment in his brother Edward's mill at Bigben Close in the north of England. Separated by ten years of age, vastly different in nature, the brothers have been alienated for ten years by a family feud. Their father, a prosperous mill owner, had failed financially six months before William's birth; and their mother—left destitute by her husband and abandoned by her aristocratic brothers because she had married beneath herself—had died giving birth to William. The boy's paternal grandparents grudgingly offer charity to William and Edward; but ten years later, when one of the boys' maternal uncles—Mr. John Seacombe—decides to stand for Parliament, he is told by the Crimsworths that they will expose his family's past heartlessness and thus ruin his hopes for a political career unless he assumes the care of William.

The Seacombes submit to the blackmail and send William to Eton, where he smarts under the burden of their niggardly charity and the insults of his brother, Edward, whose infrequent letters never fail to express his hatred for the Seacombes and to reproach William for living at their expense. Shortly after leaving Eton, William has an interview with his Seacombe uncles, who promise him a living if he enters the church and who suggest that such a career will fit him for marriage with one of his Seacombe cousins. When he refuses the offer, he is scornfully asked by his uncles if he plans like his father before him to make business his career. Angered by his uncles' sarcasm, William makes an instantaneous decision to follow precisely this course. He writes to Edward, now a successful businessman, who grudgingly agrees to employ him as a clerk in his mill in Bigben Close.

Edward, initially cold, becomes brutal when William, with an air of aristocratic aloofness, competently performs all the tasks assigned to him. For his part, William hates Edward and finds work dull and life lonely; yet having vowed to succeed as a tradesman, he ignores both his own desire to rebel and the urgings of Edward's enemy, Yorke Hunsden, that he do so. Then one day, Edward, who has been publicly embarrassed by Hunsden over his treatment of his brother, turns on William—who, he believes, has betrayed him— and threatens him with a whip. Coolly deflecting Edward's blows, William announces his decision to leave, for he is now satisfied that no weakness of will is involved in doing so. When William later meets Hunsden and accuses him of having deprived him of his means of making a living, Hunsden urges him to try his fortunes in Brussels and gives him a letter of introduction to a man of that city.

Delighting in his new-found freedom, William goes to Brussels, and with the aid of Hunsden's acquaintance, he quickly gains a position as an English teacher in a boys' school owned and run by M. Pelet. Settling into his new duties with minimal difficulty, William is soon offered additional work as a part-time teacher in Mlle. Zoraïde Reuter's school for girls that is immediately adjacent to Pelet's academy. William quickly becomes attracted to the seductive Zoraïde, and Pelet good-naturedly teases him about his interest in his new employer.

One evening while leaning out of his bedroom window and observing the garden of the girl's school, where that afternoon he enjoyed an encouraging *tête-à-tête* with Zoraïde, William overhears a conversation between her and Pelet which reveals that the two are engaged and have been secretly laughing at him while they encouraged him to fall in love with her. Infuriated by the double treachery and angry at himself for having entertained any interest in Zoraïde, William becomes openly hostile to her; and she—first surprised, then intrigued by his cold invulnerability—begins to fall in love with him. Hoping to increase his interest in her, she pretends a kindly concern for a young English-Swiss woman, Frances Evans Henri, who has taught sewing at the school and who wishes to improve her command of English in order to better her position. Zoraïde urges William to accept Frances into his class; but because he is determined to make Zoraïde suffer, he responds icily to this pupil who is thrust upon him until he becomes aware of the girl's intelligence, which is far superior to the other students' sottish stupidity. A friendship develops between Frances and William, but it is disrupted by the jealous Zoraïde, who dismisses Frances and untruthfully tells William she does not know where the girl has gone. Angered by this last evidence of Zoraïde's deceitfulness, William resigns his position at her school.

Frances sends William payment for her lessons; and determined to give her back this money, William seeks her throughout the city—finally discovering her at the grave of her aunt who had been her only remaining relative and who has only recently died. He accompanies Frances home and finds more than ever to admire in her quiet intelligence and stoicism. He knows he is falling in love, but he is kept from declaring his affection both by his fear of frightening Frances by too abrupt a change from professor to lover and by his knowledge that he lacks means to support her.

His financial situation becomes even more desperate when, finding that Pelet and Zoraïde are soon to be married, he decides he must resign his position in Pelet's school because he fears that he will become involved against his will in an illicit affair with Zoraïde if he shares a house with her. Weeks pass, and William sees nothing of Frances while he struggles to find another position. At last, although he hates to be under obligation to anyone, he calls upon a man who has long wished to aid him in gratitude for having saved his son's life. With this man's help, William gets a new position as a teacher; and he then proposes to and is accepted by Frances.

Hunsden, who has heard from his Brussels' acquaintance about William's involvement with Zoraïde, arrives in Brussels on a tour. He begins to taunt William for having indulged in the hopeless fantasy that Zoraïde would marry him, and he proceeds to accuse him of being embittered by his loss of her. To tease Hunsden, William tells him he has become engaged to a humble lace-mender. He then introduces Hunsden to Frances and laughs at Hunsden's surprise when he discovers that Frances is a well-educated, attractive young lady. Frances and William marry, and the last chapter of the book relates how, after ten years of labor, they achieve sufficient economic security to retire to England with their young son, Victor.

II *Self-Imprisonment*

The tripartite structure of *The Professor* chronicles the steps by which William Crimsworth, a man thwarted by both his actively hostile environment and the defects of his own character, gains knowledge of his world and himself; learns to control both; and through this knowledge and this control, discovers how to satisfy the deepest needs of his own nature. In recounting the details of William's past and in describing his experiences at Bigben Close, the first, brief section of the novel discloses what appears to be an insuperable problem. Like all of Charlotte's protagonists, William is an orphan in an, at best, indifferent and, at worst, inimical society. The fate of his mother, with whom he feels a bond of affinity, serves as an ominous reminder that those who displease the powerful, find "little hope or comfort"[1] in this world. And William's decision to reject the contemptuously offered help of his rich and callous uncles not only creates an "irreparable breach" (P, 4) between himself and the Seacombes, but also drives him into the purview of his successful but brutal brother, Edward, who—when he finds that he cannot cow the younger, more aristocratic man—abandons his pose of indifference to him and succumbs to homicidal rage: "I wish you were a dog! I'd set-to this minute and never stir from the spot till I'd cut every strip of flesh from your bones with this whip" (P, 40).

William's misery at Bigben Close is, however, also self-induced: a well-educated young man, William is free to leave Edward's employ and thus to escape the social degradation and the taunting cruelty he daily suffers as a menial clerk in a mill. He hates his brother; he knows that his work, dull in itself, is bringing about "the rust and cramp of [his] best faculties"; and he admits a "panting desire for freer and fresher scenes" (P, 26). Yet for three months he does not attempt to change his condition, and his reasons for refusing to do so provide evidence of his dangerous moral and psychological immaturity. William decides to remain and suffer—to endure (P, 12, 26, 37)—because he, like Jane Eyre, desires to prove himself not merely equal but superior to those holding power in the society he scorns and that scorns him.

Specifically, William feels threatened by his brother, whose physical strength far excels his, who has gained economic success, and who enjoys as the spoils of victory a palatial home and a beautiful wife. Conceiving his relationship with Edward as a battle which will elevate the victor to a position of tyranny and reduce his opponent to the condition of a "slave," William doubts his competence to meet the coming test: "Had I then force of mind to cope with him? I did not know; I had never been tried" (P, 12). Yet William's pride demands that he accept the challenge implicit in his situation; and because he defines "force of mind" as the ability to "endure for a time" and to "subdue" his feelings of "disgust" (P, 12), his plan for victory consists of maintaining a stoic indifference which he believes will prove to others his moral and intellectual superiority:

I had an instinctive feeling that it would be folly to let one's temper effervesce often with such a man as Edward. I said to myself, "I will place my cup under this continual dropping; it shall stand there still and steady; when full, it will run over of itself—meantime patience. . . ." As to the fact of my brother assuming towards me the bearing of a proud, harsh master, the fault is his, not mine; and shall his injustice, his bad feeling, turn me at once aside from the path I have chosen? No; at least, ere I deviate, I will advance far enough to see whither my career tends. As yet I am only pressing in at the entrance—a strait gate enough; it ought to have a good terminus. (P, 16–17)

Clearly, William's response to life is essentially negative; and the novel's Christian framework, established by William's frequent use of religious references in his first-person narrative, implies the inadequacy of this attitude. In describing himself as pressing in at a "strait gate," William makes use of the image Christ chooses to describe the entrance to spiritual salvation. But Christ's command to those who wish to enter upon this path is explicit: "whatsoever ye would that men should do, do ye also even so to them: for this is the law and the prophets" (Matt. 7:12–14). And this injunction William totally ignores; he satisfies himself with the belief that his only need is to protect himself, which he does by retreating into a defensive passivity.

Like Lucy Snowe, he takes pride in his stoic endurance and binds all of his energy to subduing his emotions. Perceiving the contemptuous coldness of his brother's initial invitation to come to Bigben Close, William "repressed all—even *mental* comment on his note—" (P, 5); and awaiting their first meeting, William finds that his "hand . . . clenched itself to repress the tremor with which impatience would fain have shaken it" (P, 6). Appalled by the bleakness of the factory world to which he has committed himself and well aware of his employer-brother's enmity, he "forced [his] eye to scrutinize this prospect, . . . forced [his] mind to dwell on it" (P, 11). Determined to remain inscrutable, to reveal nothing of his actual feelings, he may wonder privately, "shall I, in conversing with [my sister-in-law], feel free to show something of my real nature" (*P*, 8); but he remains a cipher in her presence, and he feels "an inward satisfaction that I had not, in the first moment of meeting [Edward], betrayed any warmth, any enthusiasm; that I had saluted this man with a quiet and steady phlegm" (*P*, 7).

Despite William's many assertions that he willfully masks his true self to test his "force of mind," it is evident that his lack of responsiveness is in large measure born of paranoid fear: "I was guarded by three faculties—Caution, Tact, Observation; and prowling and prying as was Edward's malignity, it could never baffle the lynx eyes of these, my natural sentinels. Day by day did his malice watch my tact, hoping it would sleep, and prepared to steal snake-like on its slumber, but tact, if it be genuine, never sleeps" (*P*, 27). Constantly on the alert against his brother's attempts to "read [his] character" and thereby launch a successful attack, William wears "a buckler of impenetrable indifference" (*P*, 19) which makes him feel "as secure against [Edward's] scrutiny as if I had on a casque with the visor down" (*P*, 17). These reiterated images of feral nature and warfare suggest William's overwhelming sense of a surrounding threat, a sense which leads him bleakly to invite rather than to avoid what he believes will inevitably be avowals of enmity; for it is, he thinks, "better to be misunderstood now than repulsed hereafter" (*P*, 18).

Yet such is not the case, as William himself discovers. Though he prides himself on his ability to have "kept the padlock of silence on [his] mental wealth" (*P*, 27) and to have suffered Edward's contemptuous treatment silently, William bears an "involuntary grudge" against Yorke Hunsden simply "because he had more than once been the tacit witness of insults offered by Edward to me. I had the conviction that he could only regard me as a poor-spirited slave, wherefore I now went about to shun his presence and eschew his conversation" (*P*, 21). Glad his appearance of "indifference" to his brother's taunts should make Edward believe he is "wasting his ammunition on a statue" (*P*, 19), William cannot help resenting the fact that the young women of Edward's social circle see him as "a block, or a piece of furniture," rather than as "an acting, thinking, sentient man" (*P*, 20).

In striving to protect himself and to prove his superiority, William has actually turned himself into his own destroyer, for he has created a situation in which he is torn by equally powerful but mutually opposed impulses and desires. His passionate longing for freedom wars with his compulsion to bow down before the "image of

Duty, the fetish of Perseverance"; his anger at what his allegiance to these two "household Gods" drives him to do to himself combines with his "antipathy" toward Edward, which "excluded [him] from every glimpse of the sunshine of life"; and he begins "to feel like a plant growing in humid darkness out of the slimy walls of a well" (*P*, 26). In retrospect, he realizes that his decision to work for Edward, which he made to salve his self-respect and which his pride keeps him from reversing, was the act of "a fool" (*P*, 3).

Trapped in this snare of his own making, William listens while "two voices [speak] within [him]; again and again they [utter] the same monotonous phrases. One [says]: 'William, your life is intolerable.' The other: 'What can you do to alter it?' " (*P*, 27). Although he "demand[s] of [his] soul" an answer to his endless questions of "Why did I make myself a tradesman? . . . Why, at dawn tomorrow, must I repair to Crimsworth's Mill?" (*P*, 36), William can find no way to release himself from his life-destroying course; and after a sleepless night, he—like the "automaton" (*P*, 32) that he has been accused of being—springs "from [his] bed with other slaves" (*P*, 36) at the summons to return to labor.

In part, William is unable to reconcile the warring aspects of his personality because, like the heroines of Charlotte's other three novels, he is afraid to do so. His cold, self-isolating responses to women are clearly the result of his fear of succumbing to a physical desire that would overpower his conscious will. He may insist that he is unmoved by what he describes as "vivacity, vanity, coquetry" and that he is "no Oriental; white necks, carmine lips and cheeks, clusters of bright curls, do not suffice for me" (*P*, 9); but his insistence is suspect since when he attends a dance, he admits, "I should have liked well enough to be introduced to some pleasing and intelligent girl"; but finding "the smiles were lavished on other eyes," he "turned away tantalized" (*P*, 20). In part, he is stymied by the fact that while he is clearly aware of what he hates, he is merely a "rebel against circumstances; . . . a fool, and know[s] not what [he] want[s]" (*P*, 11). His "darling, . . . cherished-in-secret, Imagination" (*P*, 26) makes him "dare to dream of congeniality, repose, and union" (*P*, 38); but the evanescence of his vision is revealed when he speaks of how he hopelessly scans female faces, searching for a "gleam of intellect," "a glimpse of soul," a "Promethean spark" (*P*, 9).

At length, William's internal tension becomes so great that his self-control snaps, although he takes pains to deny that this is, in fact, what has happened. The mysterious Yorke Hunsden, who has pierced William's defensive mask, scorns his mode of behavior, saying, "when a man endures patiently what ought to be unendurable, he is a fossil" (P, 32). Moreover, William himself must admit that his stance has achieved nothing positive: his "aspirations spread eager wings towards a land of visions," but still he "toil[s] like a slave" at a "task [as] thankless and bitter as that of the Israelite crawling over the sun-baked fields of Egypt in search of straw and stubble wherewith to accomplish his tale of bricks" (P, 38). He knows he can attain nothing but his own destruction in his tyrant-brother's infernal mill, "vomiting soot from its iron bowels" (P, 13). Yet William despises the temptation to quit—such an act being, he believes, a defeat, for his vaunted "endurance" "is not four months old" (P, 37).

In consequence, William goads Edward into physically attacking him; and having defended himself, he proceeds to use the open rupture as an excuse to escape "without injury to [his] self-respect" (P, 43). His rebellion is, in fact, as he admits after he has committed it, an act of self-preservation. In attempting to prove his manhood, he had come perilously close to losing his soul—to becoming a "statue" (P, 19), a "block" (P, 20), a "fossil," an "automaton" (P, 32); now the sudden release of pent-up emotion revivifies him—"a warm excited thrill ran through my veins, my blood seemed to give a bound, and then raced fast and hot along its channels" (P, 40). Suddenly, he perceives, "Life was again open to me" (P, 43); and he leaves Bigben Close for Belgium, feeling himself new-born: "My sense of enjoyment possessed an edge whetted to the finest, untouched, keen, exquisite. I was young; I had good health; pleasure and I had never met; no indulgence of hers had enervated or sated one faculty of my nature. Liberty I clasped in my arms for the first time, and the influence of her smile and embrace revived my life like the sun and the west wind" (P, 54).

III   *Temptation*

In the second section of *The Professor*, which occurs in Brussels, William discovers that a surrender to passion not only is dangerous, but also will not secure the elusive prize he seeks. As the garden imagery which runs through the novel implies, William must undergo a series of temptations, a time of testing; for as Charlotte notes

in her preface, he is "Adam's son" and must "share Adam's doom."
In isolating himself from others, he has hidden his true nature even
from himself and thus remains ignorant of the perilous strength of
his sensual impulses. Therefore, William is unprepared for the trial
before him in Brussels. Entering the door of his new employer, M.
Pelet, he notes the house opposite bears a sign reading "Pensionnat
de Demoiselles," and the word "Pensionnat" "excite[s] an uneasy
sensation in [his] mind." As he gazes at the school, some of the girls
step forth. He looks for "a pretty face amongst them, but their close,
little French bonnets hid their features; in a moment they were
gone" (*P*, 59).

This single and seemingly insignificant conjunction of male sensu-
ality and an image of concealed beauty sets the tone for what follows:
within the walls of the *pensionnat*, as William soon discovers, lies an
inaccessible, green, and secret garden; and the hazards which bar its
entrance become the physical counterpart of William's sexual inexperience and lack of self-knowledge born of emotional repression:

M. Pelet conducted me to my apartment. . . . one of [the] windows was
boarded up. . . . M. Pelet . . . explained:
    "La fenêtre fermée donne sur un jardin appartenant à un pensionnat de
demoiselles," said he, "et les convenances exigent—enfin, vous com-
prenez— n'est-ce pas, Monsieur?"
    "Oui, oui," was my reply, and I looked of course quite satisfied; but when
M. Pelet had retired and closed the door after him, the first thing I did was
to scrutinize closely the nailed boards, hoping to find some chink or crevice
which I might enlarge, and so get a peep at the consecrated ground. My
researches were vain, for the boards were well joined and strongly nailed. It
is astonishing how disappointed I felt. (*P*, 64)

Left alone, William crouches at the sealed window, hunting for an
opening through which he can spy on the unsuspecting "demoiselles"; but the true cause of his frenzied agitation he conceals from
himself as completely as the boarded-up window conceals the sight
of the girls in the garden of the *pensionnat*. Unaware of his obses-
sion with sexual matters, he titillates his imagination by projecting
his own appetites onto others: he suspects M. Pelet, whose actions
give no grounds for such suspicion, of "a degree of laxity in his code
of morals, [because] there was something so cold and *blasé* in his
tone whenever he alluded to what he called, 'le beau sexe.' "
Though he insists that he "abhor[s], from [his] soul, mere licen-

tiousness" (P, 69), William entertains the lascivious fantasy that Mr.
Pelet's ancient, slatternly mother has invited him to tea in order to
provide herself the opportunity to avow her love for him:

Just as I laid my hand on the handle of the dining-room door, a queer idea
glanced across my mind.
   "Surely she's not going to make love to me," said I. "I've heard of old
Frenchwomen doing odd things in that line; and the goûter? They generally
begin such affairs with eating and drinking, I believe." (P, 71)

Inexperienced and vulnerable, William moves toward his meeting with Zoraïde. Unlike M. Pelet's mother, Zoraïde Reuter is not
an illusory danger conjured by the imagination but a real and for-
midable adversary. She threatens William far more than his uncles
and his brother, because her power is grounded in William's desire
for her; this enemy works within the gates. At their very first meeting, Zoraïde holds out the promise of fulfillment: ". . . you have not
seen [the garden] yet, . . . come to the window and take a better
view." The woman who opens the window on the "enclosed de-
mesne" which for William had "hitherto been . . . an unknown region" is no perfumed seductress. William turns from the garden to
Zoraïde and sees "a little and roundly formed woman . . . as fair as a
fair Englishwoman . . . ; her hair was nut-brown, and she wore it in
curls. . . . there was a certain serenity of eye, and freshness of complexion, most pleasing to behold." Yet the dangers of Zoraïde's
charm are implicit in William's description of her: "The colour on
her cheek was like the bloom on a good apple, which is as sound at
the core as it is red on the rind" (P, 78–79). She is the perilous apple
of the secret garden.
   William's susceptibility to Zoraïde is obvious: at their first meeting, he acknowledges, "I would rather have sat a little longer; what
had I to return to but my small empty room? And my eyes had
pleasure in looking at Mdlle Reuter" (P, 80). Although it becomes
increasingly difficult for him to turn from the pleasures of her company to the tedium of his solitary existence, William struggles
against capitulation. While entertaining desires he has never dared
to acknowledge, he still retains something of his old aloofness. He
had defeated his uncles and brother by restraining his emotions;
now he attempts to subdue Zoraïde through his powers of intellect.
Creating a wall of reserve which even his emotions cannot assail,

William consciously and with some skill plays the game through which Mr. Duffy in James Joyce's "A Painful Case" blunders:

> . . . she wanted to know where her mind was superior to mine—by what feeling or opinion she could lead me.
> I enjoyed the game much, and did not hasten its conclusion; sometimes I gave her hopes, beginning a sentence rather weakly, when her shrewd eye would light up—she thought she had me; having led her a little way, I delighted to turn round and finish with sound, hard sense, whereat her countenance would fall. (*P*, 90)

> I believe she thought I was like a smooth and bare precipice, which offered neither jutting stone nor tree-root, nor tuft of grass to aid the climber. . . . I found it at once pleasant and easy to evade all [her] efforts; it was sweet, when she thought me nearly won, to turn round and to smile in her very eyes, half scornfully, and then to witness her scarcely veiled, though mute mortification. (*P*, 107)

But William's strategy fails to take his own weakness into account. Defeated in her every attempt to scale the fortress of his reserve, Zoraïde extends her "small and white hand"—and William succumbs: "I met her eye too in full—obliging her to give me a straightforward look; this last test went against me: it left her as it found her—moderate, temperate, tranquil; me it disappointed" (*P*, 90). Thus William enters the garden of experience as Zoraïde enters his heart: "her finger, essaying, proving every atom of the casket, touched its secret spring, and for a moment the lid sprung open; she laid her hand on the jewel within" (*P*, 107). Later, in the mysterious garden, Zoraïde "raised herself on her tip-toes, and, plucking a beautiful branch of lilac, offered it to [him] with grace"; and William, who accepts the trophy, is "satisfied for the present, and hopeful for the future" (*P*, 109).

William reaches the midpoint of his ascent up the "Hill of Difficulty" when he succumbs to passion and rejects his own standards. Knowing that Zoraïde may "be truly deficient in sound principle" (*P*, 111), he still considers marriage, and concludes, "It seemed as if the romantic visions my imagination had suggested of this garden, while it was yet hidden from me by the jealous boards, were more than realized" (*P*, 109). In truth, William wanders in a labyrinth of deception; he has placed himself in the very peril from which his former aloofness was intended to protect him. Having committed himself emotionally, he is now open to betrayal; he overhears Zoraïde and M. Pelet walking in the garden, overhears their plans to marry, overhears Zoraïde's "little laugh of exulting coquetry" when the jealous M. Pelet accuses her of successfully capturing William's heart, and overhears Zoraïde dismiss himself as "an unknown foreigner" who cannot "bear comparison with [Pelet] either physically or mentally" (P, 113).

Zoraïde's rebuff provokes William's worst fears and increases the difficulty of his search for the ideal woman with whom he will find "congeniality, repose, union." In The Professor, as in Charlotte's other novels, she insists that her protagonists will find peace only when they discover their true soul mate—the one individual in all the world who perfectly complements the protagonist's personality, satisfying it intellectually, morally, spiritually, and sexually—the one individual who can remove the protagonist's sense of isolation. Although Zoraïde's charms obscure and distort William's vision of his ideal, her betrayal shocks him into an awareness that she lacks the "Promethean spark" which he seeks: "There is metal there. . . . Would that there were fire also, living ardour to make the steel glow—then I could love her" (P, 118).

William retreats once more into bitter and sterile aloofness. Insisting in one breath that "God knows I am not by nature vindictive; I would not hurt a man because I can no longer trust or like him" (P, 115), he scornfully turns on Zoraïde at their next encounter: "meeting her gaze full, arresting, fixing her glance, I shot into her eyes, from my own, a look, where there was no respect, no love, no tenderness, no gallantry; where the strictest analysis could detect nothing but scorn, hardihood, irony. I made her bear it, and feel it; her steady countenance did not change, but her colour rose, and she approached me as if fascinated" (P, 117). And, moreover, he transfers his hostility to Zoraïde's protégée, Frances Evans Henri, thus further impeding the development of a relationship with the girl who is in truth his soul mate. Although he is drawn by the "strength and rarity" of Frances' "faculties" (P, 141–42) and although he sees in her the qualities of "diligence and perseverance" (P, 177) which have been his own deities, he retains a sense of superiority which protects him from committing himself to another human being. Her attraction for him, at this stage of their relationship, resides largely in the fact that her deference salves the wounds which Zoraïde's scornful rejection of him created (P, 152–53).

Indeed, the language with which he describes their relationship reveals his unwillingness and inability to see Frances as a woman: "To speak truth, I watched [her] change much as a gardener watches the growth of a precious plant, and I contributed to it too, even as the said gardener contributes to the development of his favourite. To me it was not difficult to discover how I could best foster my pupil, cherish her starved feelings, and induce the outward manifestation of that inward vigour which sunless drought and blighting-blast had hitherto forbidden to expand" (*P*, 154).

When Frances is hurriedly dismissed from her position at Zoraïde's school and disappears, William, still immured in cold pride, makes no effort to find her until his pride itself provokes him into doing so. He resolves to "seek her through Brussels" (*P*, 171) only when she sends him the money she owes for her English lessons. While he was her benefactor, she was not his equal; but by paying him, she asserts her independence, and William determines to subjugate her pride in order to elevate his own: "If she had offered me [the coins in person, instead of sending them], I could have thrust them back into her little hand, and shut up the small, taper fingers over them—so—and compelled her shame, her pride, her shyness, all to yield to a little bit of determined Will" (*P*, 170).

William's relationship with Frances is additionally impeded by his ambivalent attitude toward Zoraïde, whose charms still lure him although he despises her; and his confusion is emphasized by his questioning search, the primary action of this section of the novel. The school and its luminous, whispering garden become a shadowy maze in which the quest for the beloved always ends in bafflement. The ruler of the maze is Zoraïde; cold, deliberate, omnipresent—the incarnation of the dangerous and attractive—she tries to sever the tenuous relationship between Frances and William, and having condemned him to a long and seemingly futile search, she tempts him to give up his quest. Significantly, when William asks directly where Frances has gone, Zoraïde replies by inviting William to "step into the garden," now rich in "summer pride" (*P*, 160); and even when she confesses her falseness and her cruelty in dismissing Frances, William is forced to admit that the "temptation [she offered] penetrated to my senses" (*P*, 163).

Like a second Eve, Zoraïde leads William into "the center of the middle alley" (*P*, 160) of the green and glowing garden. There—under "the embowering branch of a huge laburnum, whose golden

flowers, blent with the dusty green leaves of a lilac-bush, formed
[an] . . . arch" (*P*, 162)—she offers the temptation that is herself:
moral death shimmering in the guise of life. His feelings for her
seem to be the first hints of a fuller, more joyful physical existence to
come; but in truth his emotions push him toward destruction, con-
demning him to the sterility of passion without love and forcing him
to embrace evil at the very moment he recognizes it. For as he finds
with a kind of horror, his once indomitable will can no longer control
his passion. Zoraïde who has sought for months to "ensnare" him, to
find the "key to [his] heart" (*P*, 162), has come close to achieving her
purpose when—driven by her own increasing sexual desire—she
abases herself before him and thus awakens his latent sadistic impulses:

I had ever hated a tyrant; and, behold, the possession of a slave, self-given,
went near to transform me into what I abhorred! There was at once a sort of
low gratification in receiving this luscious incense from an attractive and still
young worshipper; and an irritating sense of degradation in the very experience of the pleasure. When she stole about me with the soft step of a slave, I
felt at once barbarous and sensual as a pasha. (*P*, 193)

Both significantly and appropriately, William's search brings him
to Frances not in Zoraïde's oppressive garden, but in a somber land
scorched by the heat of a dying summer: "Passing up the avenue I
saw objects on each hand which, in their own mute language of
inscription and sign, explained clearly to what abode I had made my
way. This was the house appointed for all living; crosses, monu-
ments, and garlands of everlastings announced, 'The Protestant
Cemetery, outside the gate of Louvain' " (*P*, 172–73). In this somber
setting, Frances stands among the insignia of death and offers the
stern love which William's condition demands. As "Adam's son,"
William must "share Adam's doom"; he must live his life not in a
"well-protected garden" but in "the house appointed for all
living"—the mutable, fallen world.
    Frances' appearance marks her as all that William has sought—
the other half of himself who takes life from his presence and who
gives to him in full measure: "I had hardly time to observe that she
was wasted and pale, ere called to feel a responsive inward pleasure
by the sense of most full and exquisite pleasure glowing in the
animated flush, and shining in the expansive light, now diffused
over [her] face. It was the summer sun flashing out after the heavy

summer shower; and what fertilizes more rapidly than that beam, burning almost like fire in its ardour?" (*P*, 176). He recognizes that she is his "lost jewel" (*P*, 175), his "treasure," his "best object of sympathy on earth" (*P*, 177).

IV *Reclamation*

Once William makes his choice, *The Professor* chronicles the steps he takes to exorcise the remnants of his destructive pride. Repudiating his former superior stance, he admits that like other men, he is open to temptation; and he resigns his position in order to avoid further contact with Zoraïde. But without a job, he cannot support Frances and cannot tell her, therefore, about his feelings; and although he searches diligently, he can find no position. Only one difficult path remains open: William, who formerly experienced perverse joy when he rejected the meager offers of his uncles and his brother, must swallow his pride and ask for help from a M. Vandenhuten, who, after William had saved his son from drowning, had promised to aid him should the need ever arise. William sees that "necessity" rather than "merit" must serve as the basis for his application to Vandenhuten, and he notes that a "request" based on such considerations "revolted my pride and contradicted my habits" (*P*, 207). Therefore, he at first attempts a compromise: he decides to humble himself sufficiently to ask for aid; but at the same time, he attempts to shelter himself in the bastion of his belief in his inner superiority:

> M. Vandenhuten was rich, respected, and influential; I, poor, despised and powerless; so we stood to the world at large as members of the world's society; but to each other, as a pair of human beings, our positions were reversed. . . . my mind having more fire and action than his, instinctively assumed and kept the predominance.
>
> This point settled, and my position well ascertained, I addressed him on the subject of my affairs. . . . (*P*, 222)

But in the very act of requesting succor, William discovers the worthlessness of his false pride; M. Vandenhuten's goodness makes him a better man than William, as William discovers: "As I exchanged a smile with him, I thought the benevolence of his truthful face was better than the intelligence of my own" (*P*, 222). The last barrier therefore falls when, applying to M. Vandenhuten, William conquers himself; and his victory miraculously subdues his world: "I

forgot fastidiousness, conquered reserve, thrust pride from me.
. . . and at the very crisis when I had tried my last effort and
knew not what to do, Fortune looked in at me one morning . . . and
threw a prize into my lap" (P, 223).

The destruction of his pride frees William from loneliness and
enables him to establish a positive human relationship. No longer
must he hate those with power; no longer must he retreat into
arrogance to save his self-esteem. He leaves his benefactor with the
words: "I do not feel an obligation irksome, conferred by your kind
hand; I do not feel disposed to shun you because you have done me
a favour; from this day you must consent to admit me to your intimate acquaintance, for I shall hereafter recur again and again to the
pleasure of your society" (P, 224). Not only has William become able
to accept affection; he has also become willing to take the ultimate
risk of asking for it; he proposes to Frances, and when Frances asks,
"Monsieur sera-t-il aussi bon mari qu'il a été bon maître?" he
answers, "I will try" (P, 236).

William's transformation enables him to conquer the destructive
forces both inside and outside himself. The physical manifestation of
his victory occurs as Hunsden accompanies him home soon after his
successful proposal to Frances:

"And that is your lace-mender?" said he; "and you reckon you have done
a fine, magnanimous thing in offering to marry her? . . . And I pitied the
fellow, thinking his feelings had misled him, and that he had hurt himself by
contracting a low match!"
"Just let go my collar, Hunsden."
On the contrary he swayed me to and fro; so I grappled him round the
waist. It was dark; the street lonely and lampless. We had then a tug for it;
and after we had both rolled on the pavement, and with difficulty picked
ourselves up, we agreed to walk on more soberly. (P, 256–57)

This strange struggle in the dark dramatically unifies the novel's
religious imagery. If Frances is William's soul mate, then
Hunsden—who throughout the novel repeatedly and mysteriously
appears and disappears and who urges William toward the garden of
temptation and Zoraïde—is William's alter ego. Establishing
"union" with Frances destroys the power of the taunting, mocking
Hunsden, who has influenced William by manipulating the destructive elements in his personality. Having urged William to break
with the factory world and to taste the dangerous delight that comes

with absolute submission to violent passion, Hunsden wrote the letter of introduction which placed William in the center of Zoraïde's garden; and in a later letter he makes overt all that William has found latently perilous in that world:

I have no doubt in the world that you are doing well in that greasy Flanders; living probably on the fat of the unctuous land; sitting like a black-haired, tawny-skinned, long-nosed Israelite by the flesh-pots of Egypt; or like a rascally son of Levi near the brass cauldrons of the sanctuary, and every now and then plunging in a consecrated hook, and drawing out of the sea of broth the fattest of heave-shoulders and the fleshiest of wave-breasts. (*P*, 202)

Significantly, the reader learns very little about Hunsden. As a character, he has no existence apart from the reactions he so skillfully produces in William, and William recognizes in Hunsden's painfully acute perceptions the powers of an alter ego. Early in the novel, William discusses his past with Hunsden; unable to "repress a half-smile" at one point in his narrative, he notes that "a similar demi-manifestation of feeling appeared at the same moment on Hunsden's lips": " 'Oh, I see!' said he, looking into my eyes, and it was evident he *did* see right down into my heart" (*P*, 48).

The religious imagery in *The Professor* makes it clear that as "Adam's son" William is doomed to be influenced by the "Old Adam" within him. Hunsden is the "Old Adam" in objective form. In the first section of the novel, William strides along the road, enraged by his brother's treatment, and meets Hunsden, who asks, "But since you're not running from the police, from whom are you running? the devil?" William's response, "On the contrary, I am going post to him" (*P*, 29), is more than a figure; for Hunsden is the diabolic principle in William's world and in William himself. Hunsden, who laughs "as mockingly, as heartlessly as Mephistopheles" (*P*, 219) and who sneers "diabolically" (*P*, 251), leads William to assert, "Were [Hunsden] the devil himself, instead of being merely very like him, I'd not condescend to get out of his way" (*P*, 203). Consequently, when William and Hunsden wrestle on the pavement and when William arises to walk on, we see acted out William's victory over the evil within himself; he has fought and thrown his personal devil.

But the full ramifications of Charlotte Brontë's theme are yet to be revealed: Hunsden does not disappear from the pages of the book; instead, he remains to remind both William and the reader what William has escaped. With Frances, William finds true happiness. Freed from the sensual temptation which Hunsden offers, William can say to him, "Bribe a seraph to fetch [you] a coal of fire from heaven . . . and with it kindle life in the tallest, fattest, most boneless, fullest-blooded of Rubens' painted women—leave me only my Alpine peri, and I'll not envy you" (P, 258). And the full extent of William's success can be gauged in the final pages of the novel. Ten years of marriage deepen and quicken the relationship of William and Frances, but Hunsden remains in the hell of his own making, which Frances early perceived:

If your world is a world without associations, Mr. Hunsden, I no longer wonder that you hate England so. I don't clearly know what Paradise is, and what angels are; yet taking it to be the most glorious region I can conceive, and angels the most elevated existence—if one of them—if Abdiel the faithful himself . . . were suddenly stripped of the faculty of association, I think he would soon rush forth from "the ever-during gates," leave heaven, and seek what he had lost in hell. (P, 250)

William's temptation and trial mark him as a type of Everyman, but his triumph does not represent the ultimate subjection of the dark forces within man; rather, his victory is emblematic of that which *every* man must struggle individually to achieve. William names his son Victor, but Victor's struggles in the inevitable battle of life must and will be desperate ones, as William himself perceives. As a father, William's duty is to prepare his son for those battles: "[Frances] sees, as I also see, a something in Victor's temper—a kind of electrical ardour and power—which emits, now and then, ominous sparks; Hunsden calls it his spirit, and says it should not be curbed. I call it the leaven of the offending Adam, and consider that it should be, if not *whipped* out of him, at least soundly disciplined" (P, 281). Victor may succeed, for he is "accessible" to "reason" and can be "infallibly subjugated" by "love." But since neither reason nor love rule Victor's world, he will also suffer: "the lad will some day get blows instead of blandishments—kicks instead of kisses; then for the fit of mute fury which will sicken his body and madden his soul; then for the ordeal of merited and salutary suffering, out of which he will come (I trust) a wiser and a better man" (P, 282).

Thus, William's fight is over, but his victory cannot be passed on to his son; it must be earned anew by every man through pain and sacrifice; and until he learns these hard lessons, the boy, like his father before him, will cherish what leads to death, not life. No longer holding power over William, Hunsden has yet remained near him; and on the last page of the novel, Hunsden's hand "rests on the boy's collar" as Hunsden "instill[s] God knows what principles into his ear" (*P*, 282). So the novel ends with William safe; but for Victor, there is no assurance of similar triumph; we know only that William's battle must be fought again by his son. Indeed, Jane Eyre, the heroine of Charlotte Brontë's second novel, is similar in character to Victor; and the struggle predicted for him is hers.

V   The Professor *and the Later Novels*

The Professor, unpublished during Charlotte's lifetime, falls below the level of aesthetic achievement of her later novels. A mixture of Angrian materials and reminiscences of her experiences in Brussels, strongly flavored with wish fulfillment, this first novel is interesting primarily because it forms a bridge between the writings of her childhood and early adulthood, and her mature work. Filled with renewed determination to write for profit and having suffered great guilt over having submitted to the control of passionate imagination, Charlotte determined when she sat down to write for the public eye to avoid, as she notes in her preface to *The Professor*, "the wild, wonderful, and thrilling—the strange, startling, and harrowing," and to deal instead with "the real." Yet passages within the novel reveal that this struggle to subdue her imaginative vision was not wholly successful. She had long been accustomed to finding imaginary Angrian scenes rising unbidden before her mind's eye; now the power that had evoked that "infernal world" played with equal force upon her memory and flooded her mind with images not of Angria but of Brussels.

But Charlotte's memories of Belgium were at best bittersweet ones; and when in *The Professor* she wrote about her past, she altered the facts to conform to her thwarted desires. She had returned from Brussels in despair; and for two years she had suffered the agony of separation from her beloved master, the happily married M. Heger. Frances Henri, the heroine of *The Professor*, whose situation and character are in many ways similar to Charlotte's own, achieves the joy denied to her creator. Frances' master, William

Crimsworth, seeing the intelligence and the passionate fire that are
to others disguised by her plain appearance, and prizing her
strength of character, is free to reject the woman who stands between him and Frances and to make her his wife. William is also in
part an aspect of Charlotte, and his successful career and ultimate
achievement of domestic happiness reverse the real events of her
life.

The choice of the point-of-view character in *The Professor* is an
indication of Charlotte's attempt to blend Angrian fantasy with reality; for William Crimsworth—as his first name, familial relationships, and character reveal—is William Percy of Angria. The feud-
ing brothers William and Edward Percy had figured as subsidiary
characters in many of Charlotte's juvenile stories, and she had pre-
viously used William as the narrative voice several times. From the
beginning, he had been conceived as a dour, proud man, and he and
his friend Charles Townshend had frequently figured as sarcastic
commentators on the perfervid Angrian social and political scene.
Much of William Percy's story, and especially those details of his
relationship with his brother, Charlotte transferred wholesale into
The Professor, with the result that at times the novel seems elliptical
and awkward: the letter to the mysterious Charles—which takes up
most of the first chapter—seems an unnecessarily confusing device
by which to fill in background; and the casual reference near the end
of the story to the fact that William "had once had the opportunity of
contemplating, near at hand, an example of the results produced by
a course of interesting and romantic domestic treachery" (*P*, 165) is
puzzling within the context of his life history as given in the novel.
Both these matters have their own origin and find their clarification
in Angrian materials: Charles is the Charles Townshend to whom
William Percy frequently wrote; the "domestic treachery" is that of
William Percy's brother-in-law, Zamorna, who consistently betrayed Percy's sister, Mary.

The amazing thing is not, of course, that Charlotte failed at this
stage of her career to smooth out the rough edges as she struggled to
join Angria and reality, but that she was able to use remnants of the
Angrian saga as effectively as she did to illuminate psychological
truth. William's fear of illicit sex, which is so awkwardly given
specific cause late in the novel, is effectively shown as a motivating
force in his character throughout, and it is the fact and effect of his
fear, rather than the reason for it, that is significant. The hostility he

feels for and meets in his brother and the fact that Charles fails even to return an answer to the letter which opens *The Professor* underline the literal and psychological alienation which is the essential of William's situation.

Charlotte wrote *Jane Eyre* during the year that *The Professor* was going its unsuccessful rounds from publisher to publisher. When, after the success of *Jane Eyre* and *Shirley*, she was casting about for another topic, she again offered this first novel to her publishers, who again rejected it. It is understandable, therefore, that both *Jane Eyre* and *Villette* bear marked similarities to *The Professor*, which she was convinced would never appear in its own right. William, Jane Eyre, and Lucy Snowe closely resemble one another: each has a sense of being at once superior and inferior to others; an awareness of being a predestined victim; a willingness to escape from torment by tormenting others; a thorny coldness, priggishness, and pride which increase alienation; and a capacity for passion which wars with the dictates of conscience.

The similarity between *The Professor* and *Jane Eyre* is not as great as that between *The Professor* and *Villette*, yet the relationship between her first two books is close enough to deserve comment. Many of the same thoughts are attributed to William and Jane—as for example, their longing for liberty and for a wider sphere of activity which is expressed in much the same way by both characters. Even more significant is the fact that both William and Jane are depicted as being motivated by pride; but while William must temper that quality to achieve happiness, Jane's very survival depends upon its unsubdued force. The similarity between *The Professor* and *Villette* in plot and setting is so marked that this first novel is often considered as merely the initial draft of the later work. While such a conclusion fails to give due weight to the manifest differences between the two works, the relationship between them is, indeed, close. Both novels express in much the same terms a hatred and fear of Roman Catholicism and of Continental culture. A considerably more important similarity is that between William and Lucy, both of whom are described again and again as having achieved a disguise of such total passivity that they are treated as insentient objects or are completely ignored by those about them.

Jane, Lucy, and William—and most particularly the latter two— are subject to the force of impulses, desires, fears, and dreams which arise from the subconscious to surprise and terrify the con-

scious self. This concept of what may be termed the layered personality, comprising the public, private, and subconscious aspects of
the self, is central to all of Charlotte's work and merges with both
the theme of masking and that of the search for the soul mate.
Surrounded by men and women who hide their true nature and
intent, the protagonists of Brontë's fiction, in order to protect themselves from prying and treacherous eyes, assume disguises which
can be penetrated only by their soul mates' spontaneous and intuitive understanding.

The nominal similarities between this first novel and Charlotte's
later work account in part for readers' lack of enthusiasm for *The
Professor:* modern critics have tended either to ignore the novel or
to dismiss it as "the work of beginner"[2] and as "lacking in artistic
unity."[3] Undoubtedly, the novel does have certain deficiencies.
Charlotte's attempt to make of her meager and unhappy experience
a story which would not only avoid Angrian excesses but would
express the stoic virtues which her rational mind espoused resulted
in an unsatisfying mixture of mundane realism and allegory, tempered with wish fulfillment. And her choice of a male character as
persona created further problems. The essential passivity and
shrinking fear of sexual experience which the narrator expresses is
the understandable, culturally induced response of a nineteenth-
century female; but attributed to a man, such attitudes convey the
impression of prudish neuroticism.

If in *The Professor* Charlotte was unable to create the amalgam of
realism and fantasy which is the hallmark of her mature work, this
novel nevertheless provides glimpses of the mastery of certain
themes and techniques which she was later to achieve. Particularly
powerful is Charlotte's evocation of the tone of perplexity, frustration, and apprehension which characterizes all of William's responses to his world. Through a series of devices, she brilliantly
conveys the impression that her hero moves amid illusory appearances which conceal a tantalizing and possibly dangerous reality. As
an English Protestant in Catholic, French-speaking Belgium, he is
confronted at every turn by impenetrable barriers to understanding.
Repeated references to the fact that he must struggle to gain and
convey knowledge in a foreign tongue and to the fact that the manners and morals of the society are antithetical to his own increase the
atmosphere of paranoid fear and confusion. These repeated references also make explicable and powerful his responses to the actual

treachery he suffers and emphasize his moral courage when he finally chooses to act self-shorn of all defenses. Though by incarnating William's alter ego in Hunsden, Charlotte sacrificed a degree of psychological complexity, she successfully conveys by other devices the deep ambivalencies of her protagonist's character. William's half-eager, half-fearful movement from his prisonlike room at Pelet's into Zoraïde's shimmering, fruitful garden, symbolizes his growth into awareness of the dangerous potential of his latent sexuality. Equally trenchant is the description of William's enthrallment by the dark specter "Hypochondria," who, after his successful proposal to Frances, takes him to her "death-cold bosom" "with arms of bone" (*P*, 241). The powerful description of his eight-day battle to repulse this "evil spirit" "as one would a dreaded and ghastly concubine coming to embitter a husband's heart towards his young bride" (*P*, 242) not only reemphasizes the pervasive intensity of William's sexual fears, but also insinuates the compelling power of the blandishments of the dark unconscious.

Thus even in this first, relatively unsuccessful novel, Charlotte reveals an ability to use plot, setting and metaphor to plumb the depths of the psyche. She had set out to tell a story that would salve her exacerbated conscience, and, indeed, the abundant religious imagery urges us to read this novel as a kind of parable. Yet *The Professor* is more than a parable. Charlotte's ability to depict emotions with great power enabled her to infuse a complex truth into her story of a fallen soul who is filled with pride and who struggles to avoid the temptations of the flesh and to achieve a love which combines passion with charity.

CHAPTER 4

Jane Eyre

I *The Plot*

JANE Eyre, an orphaned child of ten, has been living since infancy with her mother's sister-in-law, Sarah Reed and Mrs. Reed's children. When Jane, who is habitually passive, attacks her brutal cousin John Reed, she is punished by being shut into the "red-room," which she believes is haunted. Shortly thereafter, she is sent to Lowood Institution, a charity school directed by the Reverend Mr. Brocklehurst. Although Jane is pleased to leave her aunt's home, she finds little to enjoy and much to suffer at Lowood. The food is poor, the discipline brutal, and the teachers more proficient at tormenting than teaching. Even so, Jane, who is eager and determined to learn, is relatively happy because she is making scholastic progress. One day, Mr. Brocklehurst visits the school, notices Jane, and accuses her before the class of being a liar and a lost soul. Believing this false accusation has robbed her of the respect that she has tried to win, Jane remains behind after class to weep. Helen Burns, a fellow student whose intelligence and stoic endurance have won Jane's respect, finds her, and after listening to Jane's highly impassioned account, takes her to the beneficent head mistress, Maria Temple. Jane benefits from Helen's temperate counsel; and consequently, she denies Brocklehurst's accusations forcefully and clearly but without frenzy to Miss Temple, who believes her.

This first crisis successfully passed, Jane settles down to uninterrupted work until spring, when a pestilence sweeps through the school and kills many of its half-starved inhabitants. Jane herself remains well, but Helen dies. Reports of the scourge make public the woeful conditions of the school. As a result, Mr. Brocklehurst is removed from power; and the new board gives authority to Miss Temple, through whose efforts Lowood becomes an admirable in-

84

stitution. Eight years pass, during which Jane becomes the top-ranking student of the school and then a teacher there; but when Miss Temple marries and leaves, Jane feels she no longer has reason to remain, and she soon obtains the position of governess at Thornfield Hall.

At Thornfield Jane enjoys more comfort and freedom than she has ever before known. Her single pupil—the young girl Adèle—is good-tempered and affectionate; Mrs. Fairfax—who is in charge of the house in the absence of the owner, Mr. Rochester—treats Jane with warmth and respect. But having left Lowood in part for fresh stimulation, Jane is bored and restless until Mr. Rochester arrives. During the following weeks, Jane and Mr. Rochester spend many happy hours in conversation. He is intrigued by his young employee's shrewd intelligence and passionate spirit; and having returned to Thornfield in despair—believing himself doomed to suffer for his past sins—he finds her innocence and integrity a balm to his spirit. Jane delights in his attention and is stimulated by the challenge he offers when he indulges in Byronic philosophizing, which she firmly argues against.

Late one night, Jane hears infernal laughter; and when she goes to the corridor to investigate, she sees smoke coming from Mr. Rochester's room. She dashes in, extinguishes the blazing bed curtains, and awakens her master. He is gloomily evasive about the cause of the fire; and Jane, who fears to probe too deeply, assumes it has been set by the odd servant, Grace Poole, whose duties are unspecified, but whom Jane has seen in the Thornfield attics.

Mr. Rochester leaves Thornfield; and Jane, who misses him sorely, finds her misery increased when she hears that he will return with a party of people among whom will be Blanche Ingram, a young beauty whom rumor says Mr. Rochester plans to marry. When the party arrives, Jane writhes at the spectacle of his courtship of Miss Ingram. One day while Mr. Rochester is out, a gypsy appears and offers to tell the fortunes of the ladies. Jane is summoned; and when the old crone predicts happiness for her, Jane recognizes Mr. Rochester in disguise. Shortly thereafter, a visitor arrives, and that night Rochester calls Jane to the attics, where she finds the stranger bleeding from a knife wound. Told by Rochester to sponge away the blood while he goes for the surgeon, Jane sits for hours, listening to snarls and growls from the next room.

The next day, Jane is called to Gateshead Hall to attend her dying

Aunt Reed. Aware that eternity lies before her, Mrs. Reed tells Jane that three years before when Jane's paternal uncle had written to Gateshead asking for information about his niece, Mrs. Reed had told him Jane was dead. Jane, whose mind is filled with thoughts of Rochester, forgives her dying aunt this act and all other past cruelties.

Jane returns to Thornfield to find that Blanche and the party are gone. After a peaceful interval in which she luxuriates in the bliss of Rochester's presence, Jane, who still believes he will marry Blanche, tearfully admits her love and then accuses him of being inferior to herself in his willingness to marry a woman he does not love. Rochester, satisfied with this proof that she has become emotionally dependent upon him, proposes; and she accepts him with joy. As the wedding day approaches, Jane is the victim of ominous dreams and fears; and the wedding ceremony is broken off when the stranger who once was wounded at Thornfield rises from the back of the church and reveals that Rochester is already married. Jane and Rochester return to Thornfield, where Rochester takes her to the attic which imprisons his mad wife, Bertha, whom he had been tricked into marrying. Rochester pleads with Jane not to abandon him and thus thrust him into the life of sin to which he insists his despair and disappointment will lead. Although her own love for him urges her to agree to become his mistress, she refuses to do so; and she flees Thornfield during the night.

With no clear destination in mind, she takes a coach to the north of England; and having forgotten her purse on the conveyance, she finds herself penniless on the barren moors. Half dead from hunger and exposure, she stumbles to the door of a lonely house. The inhabitants, two sisters and a brother, take her in; and the brother, Reverend St. John Rivers, finds her a position as the village schoolmistress. He discovers she is his cousin and the heiress to a legacy of twenty thousand pounds left her by her paternal uncle. Jane, who has grown to love the sisters and to respect St. John, shares the fortune with them.

St. John has dedicated his life to the service of God and, despite the pleas of his sisters, is determined to go as a missionary to India. Perceiving in Jane a strong, passionate spirit which he believes endangers her immortal soul, St. John insists that Jane accompany him as his wife and serve in the mission field. Jane considers going, although she believes doing so will kill her. The misery she suffers as a result of her separation from Rochester makes her vulnerable to the power of St. John's cold but strong will. Although she attempts to refuse St. John, she is on the very verge of accepting his proposal when she hears a voice calling her name. This voice seems to be Rochester's, and she at once turns from St. John, determined to seek and to find the man she still so passionately loves.

Jane returns to Thornfield to find a blackened ruin and to hear that Rochester has been blinded and maimed in his fruitless attempt to save his wife who had escaped from her cell and had set fire to the house. Rochester now lives at Ferndean, and there Jane finds him. The two lovers are reunited as Rochester confesses his undying love for and dependence upon Jane.

II *Society, Alienation, and Isolation*

As this summation of the plot indicates, *Jane Eyre* traces an individual's desperate struggle against almost insuperable odds to establish and maintain a sense of her own identity and to satisfy the deepest needs of her nature. As Jane comes to know herself and her world, she realizes her full dilemma: free to choose and compelled to do so, she again and again finds that the course she pursues leads only to the spiritual destruction she has sought to avoid. Her consternation when she realizes her situation is communicated with special intensity because there is no ironic distance between Jane and her creator, both of whom share the same vision of the world. As G. Armour Craig points out, "the power of the 'I' of this novel is secret, undisclosable, absolute. There are no terms to explain its dominance, because no terms can appear which are not under its dominance."[1]

Ultimately, Jane solves her problem by acting upon her selfish decision that contrary to the dictates of society and the teaching of religion, her own needs must be satisfied. In the context of Jane's account, this decision is justified by the desperate nature of her situation: Jane is compelled to reply only upon herself, to work out her destiny alone, and to do so in an environment which is not only totally hostile to her but which is convulsive and chaotic in itself. On all sides there is evidence that the bonds which traditionally tie individuals together have been ruptured by malignant circumstance or by man's innately evil nature.

Pestilence-stricken Lowood, the first of the dark labyrinths Jane must thread, is a monument to the destruction of the most basic human unit, the family: "all the girls here have lost either one or both parents, and this is called an institution for educating orphans."[2] Gateshead Hall rising somberly out of a winter landscape of "leafless shrubbery" and offering its inmates a view "of wet lawn and storm-beat shrub, with ceaseless rain sweeping away wildly before a long and lamentable blast" (JE, I, 1–2), presents a far wilder scene within as the Reed family relationship, once merely unpleasant, degenerates into cold hatred and maddened recollection. Eliza turns on her sister and swears, "I can tell you this—if the whole human race, ourselves excepted, were swept away, and we two stood alone on the earth, I would leave you in the old world, and betake myself to the new" (JE, I, 306). And in the darkened room above, Mrs. Reed dies attended only by images of guilt, blood, and violent death, which her mad pride cannot dispel:

John does not at all resemble his father, and I am glad of it: John is like me and like my brothers. . . . Oh, I wish he would cease tormenting me with letters for money! I have no more money to give him. . . . He threatens me—he continually threatens me with his own death, or mine: and I dream sometimes that I see him laid out with a great wound in his throat, or with a swollen and blackened face. I am come to a strange pass: I have heavy troubles. (JE, I, 301)

Thornfield Hall to which Jane journeys in search of "real, knowledge of life" (JE, I, 105), harbors the most conclusive evidence of the danger implicit in all passional human relationships. In the lower corridors of the manor house is heard the laughter of Adéle, the legacy of a union which ended in "screams, hysterics, prayers, protestations, convulsions" (JE, I, 185). And above, in one of the "mystic cells" of the sinister third story, rages the "crime . . . that live[s] incarnate in [the] sequestered mansion"—the demon-voiced "creature . . . , masked in an ordinary woman's face and shape" (JE, I, 271–72), in whose conjugal embrace, Edward Fairfax Rochester found all hope extinguished.

The sense of the deadly hostility of this world is strengthened still more by the fact that isolation is seen throughout the novel as the normal, although difficult, lot of humanity. Diana and Mary Rivers are driven from Moor House by economic necessity and are forced to "earn the dependent's crust among strangers" (JE, II, 151). Helen Burns, realizing her difference from those about her, gratefully escapes from a lonely past and a dangerous future: "I leave no one to regret me much. . . . By dying young I shall escape great sufferings. I had not qualities or talents to make my way very well in the world: I should have been continually at fault" (*JE*, I, 101). Bound by a harsh Calvinistic creed, St. John Rivers rejects all human ties: he turns from the beautiful Rosamond, who loves him; and determined to serve God as a missionary, he "considers himself an alien from his native country—not only for life, but in death" (*JE*, II, 151–52). Having found a demon where he sought a bride, Mr. Rochester "transformed [himself] into a Will-o'-the-wisp" and "pursued wanderings as wild as those of the March-spirit" (*JE*, II, 93) until having come at last to regard fruitful human companionship as a dream, he lives imprisoned in himself, a man "in a harsh, bitter, frame of mind, the result of a useless, roving, lonely life—corroded with disappointment, sourly disposed against all men, and especially against all *woman*kind" (*JE*, II, 95–96).

Jane's sense of her physical and spiritual isolation is, therefore, neither neurotic illusion nor the product of singular circumstances; rather, it represents the human condition. The Everyman of her world, Jane repeatedly sees herself and is seen by the reader as a solitary pilgrim. In the half-light of the "red-room," she awakens to spiritual consciousness—consciousness of her alien state—when she looks into the mirror and sees the "glittering eyes" of a "strange little figure," "like one of the tiny phantoms, half fairy, half imp," which "evening stories represented as coming up out of lone, ferny dells" (*JE*, I, 11). Descriptions of Jane's travels emphasize her alienation: she is "severed from Bessie and Gateshead" and "whirled away to [the] unknown, . . . remote and mysterious regions" (*JE*, I, 48) of Lowood; she journeys to an enigmatic future at Thornfield with the awareness that she is "quite alone in the world: cut adrift from every connection" (*JE*, I, 117); fleeing Rochester, she wanders through the pathless, darkened moors, tormented by the thought that "not a tie holds me to human society . . . —not a charm or hope calls me where my fellow-creatures are" (*JE*, II, 110).

Tableaulike scenes constantly emphasize Jane's isolation: forever an outcast, she is seen as a lonely child leaning over the Gateshead banister to catch the "sound of the piano or the harp played below" as an accompaniment to the gaiety from which she "was, of course, excluded" (*JE*, I, 30); later, she is pictured as a diminutive figure in black who watches "the servants passing backwards and forwards," as she strains to distinguish the notes of a duet from her vantage point in the darkness at the top of the Thornfield staircase (*JE*, I, 216). Intensifying these descriptions of physical separation is Jane's oppressive knowledge of a deep and terrifying spiritual loneliness which she reveals both in her hallucinatory paintings of drowning strugglers overwhelmed amid vast seas and in her sudden realization, when she learns of the gravity of Helen Burns' condition, that the individual soul is trapped in a meaningless and turbulent universe rushing toward ruin: ". . . my mind made its first earnest effort to comprehend what had been infused into it concerning heaven and hell: . . . and for the first time glancing behind, on each side, and before it, it saw all round an unfathomed gulf: it felt the one point where it stood—the present; all the rest was formless cloud and vacant depth: and it shuddered at the thought of tottering, and plunging amid that chaos" (*JE*, I, 98).

III   *The Dangers and Attractions of Love*

Filled with this sense of the self standing alone and poised above a gulf of nothingness, Jane frantically seeks to unite herself with some other being through love; and when her desire to give and to receive love is frustrated, she feels threatened by the destruction she fears. Unable to bear any longer the cruel alienation that Mrs. Reed forces upon her, she turns on her aunt, saying, "You think I have no feelings, and that I can do without one bit of love or kindness; but I cannot live so" (*JE*, I, 41). Her fear that Mr. Brocklehurst's unjust accusation has made her an object of derision leads to the wild cry, "If others don't love me, I would rather die than live—I cannot bear to be solitary and hated" (*JE*, I, 84); and when she believes that Rochester's marriage to Blanche Ingram is imminent, she sees "the necessity of departure [from Thornfield]; and it is like looking on the necessity of death" (*JE*, II, 17). During the period of her betrothal to Rochester, she remarks that her "thin crescent-destiny seemed to enlarge; the blanks of existence were filled up; my bodily health improved" (*JE*, I, 188); and her impending separation from her lover deprives her, as she perceives, of life itself: "Jane Eyre, who had been an ardent, expectant woman—almost a bride—was a cold, solitary girl again: her life was pale, her prospects were desolate. A Christmas frost had come at midsummer; a white December storm had whirled over June; ice glazed the ripe apples, drifts crushed the blowing roses; on hay-field and corn-field lay a frozen shroud" (*JE*, II, 74).

That love is, as Jane's statements assert, the power which sustains life, is made obvious by the fact that both Helen Burns and St. John Rivers, who fear the consequences of a fully developed emotional response, virtually will their own destruction. Jane hysterically declares, "I cannot bear to be solitary and hated," and she protests that to gain "some real affection from . . . any . . . whom I truly love, I would willingly submit to have the bone of my arm broken," but Helen dismisses Jane's outburst with the cool words, "You think too much of the love of human beings" (*JE*, I, 84–85). Denying both the supreme importance of human relationships and the overwhelming power of passion, Helen tranquilly accepts her "gentle and gradual illness" as an escape from the "great sufferings" which life entails (*JE*, I, 101). St. John Rivers' position is, of course, more extreme than Helen's. His tumultuous love for Rosamond forces him to respond, and for a "little space" of time, he "rested [his] temples on the breast of temptation, and put [his] neck voluntarily under her yoke of flowers." But almost at once he suppresses his desire, for he believes that "there is an asp in the garland: . . . her promises are hollow—her offers false" (*JE*, II, 178). He fears the "wild intensity" of a love which would lure him from the band of men who seek only the mansions of heaven and which would imprison him forever "at [his] bride Rosamond Oliver's feet" (*JE*, II, 177); he dreads the emotion that is to him a disease, a "delirium and delusion" (*JE*, II, 178), "a mere fever of the flesh" (*JE*, II, 180). And so he speeds to his waiting death anticipating not earthly satisfaction but an "incorruptible crown": "My master . . . has forewarned me. Daily he announces more distinctly,—'Surely I come quickly!' and hourly I more eagerly respond,—'Amen; even so come, Lord Jesus!' " (*JE*, II, 284).

Out of fear, perplexity, or unwillingness to prolong what seems a futile struggle for happiness, Jane at times entertains life-destroying attitudes. Aware that she is "a discord in Gateshead Hall" (*JE*, I, 13), she attempts to disguise her innate differences from the Reeds; and in an effort to escape the torments they are eager to visit upon her as an alien interloper, for ten years she is "patient and quiescent under any treatment" (*JE*, I, 311). Eager for success at Lowood, she adopts the pattern of behavior which will win her praise in that regimented and disciplined world, and her success at such playacting is obvious when she claims that "to the eyes of others, usually even to my own, I appeared a disciplined and subdued character"

(*JE*, I, 104). Driven by her sense that she must flee from Mr. Rochester, she is capable of renouncing "love and Idol" (*JE*, II, 100), although she tells herself to do so is suicide: "you shall tear yourself away, none shall help you: you shall, yourself, pluck out your right eye: yourself cut off your right hand; your heart shall be the victim; and you, the priest, to transfix it" (*JE*, II, 76). And she is capable of continuing to pursue this course. Even though she sees only a crushing imprisonment—a living death—in the future which St. John almost forces upon her, she must admit her ability to bear that "iron shroud": "I *can* do what he wants me to do: I am forced to see and acknowledge that" (*JE*, II, 218–19).

Indeed, at this point in her career, Jane is tempted by the release which death would offer. Believing that without Rochester her life is "valueless" (*JE*, II, 120), Jane loses her desire to live; and existing in such a devitalized state, she falls subject to the "awful charm" (*JE*, II, 216) of St. John's power and nearly submits to his demand that she enter into a loveless marriage, even though she insists, "If I were to marry you, you would kill me. You are killing me now" (*JE*, II, 230). The cold, austere pattern which St. John's "shaping hand" would impose upon her "vague," "diffuse" (*JE*, II, 218) life so fascinates Jane that she is helpless to oppose the "certain influence . . . that [takes] away [her] liberty of mind" (*JE*, II, 210), although she knows that as a victim of this "freezing spell," she must "more and more . . . disown half [her] nature, stifle half [her] faculties" (*JE*, II, 211). Despite her terrified admission, "Alas! If I join St. John, I abandon half myself: if I go to India, I go to premature death" (*JE*, II, 219), she is tempted to give up the struggle against him—to "rush down the torrent of his will into the gulf of his existence, and there lose my own" (*JE*, II, 238).

Thus one half of Jane's position is clarified and the conditions of one of her possible choices are revealed. But if refusing to establish strong emotional ties destines one to destruction, accepting the full burden of love is equally perilous.[3] Neither Helen nor St. John denies human attachments without reason: both see clearly the danger implicit in an absolute surrender to a passion that may usurp reason and commit one irrevocably to inner chaos. The dark and brutal London where John Reed becomes a profligate drunkard and the glittering, hectic Paris where Rochester is betrayed by his mistress, Céline Varens, are the outposts of a world whose essential,

secret, and virulent center is the "tapestried room" (*JE*, II, 70) of
Thornfield. There, hidden among a maze of "narrow, low, and dim"
passages, behind one of a series of "small, black doors" (*JE*, II, 135),
shrouded by a shadowy "antique" (*JE*, I, 185) drapery, is the "secret
inner cabinet," the "goblin's cell" (*JE*, II, 92). And within it rages
the "mystery" that breaks out "now in fire and now in blood, at the
deadest hours of the night" (I, 272)—the raving fiend to which
Rochester, "dazzled, stimulated," his "senses . . . excited" (*JE*, II,
86), bound himself while the West Indian moon "threw her last
bloody glance over a world quivering with the ferment of tempest"
(*JE*, II, 90). The snarling, "black and scarlet" (*JE*, II, 93) visage of
mad Bertha Mason is the ultimate image of uncontrollable passion.
She is last described standing on the battlements of Thornfield, the
manor house that she has animated with her spirit. Silhouetted
against the night sky, her "long, black hair . . . streaming against
the flames" (*JE*, II, 252) of the fire which she has set and which will
consume her, she becomes an emblem of the self-destructive power
of totally unrestrained emotion.

No less than Bertha, Jane is subject to this danger: her intense
desire for love leads her to insist wildly that to gain "real affection"
from one of whom she is truly fond, "I would willingly . . . stand
behind a kicking horse, and let it dash its hoof at my chest" (*JE*, I,
85). Moreover, her lapses into emotional frenzy suggest a latent
instability: she flies at John Reed like a "desperate thing" (*JE*, I, 6);
she so violently resists the efforts of Bessie and Miss Abbot to subdue her that they "darkly" stare on her as if "incredulous of [her]
sanity" (*JE*, I, 9); and when she turns in defiance on the mistress of
Gateshead, her voice is "savage, high," and she "tremble[s] . . . violently," "thrilled with ungovernable excitement" (*JE*, I, 41–42).

Like Bertha, the ravager of Thornfield who is described as being a
"wild beast" and a "fury" (*JE*, I, 272), Jane is seen by her enemies as
a "fury" (*JE*, I, 7) and a "mad cat" (*JE*, I, 8). Forced to live what she
considers a "monotonous life" (*JE*, I, 147), Jane longs with hysterical
intensity for emotional release, for an experience which will corre-
spond with her fantasies: "the restlessness was in my nature; it
agitated me to pain sometimes. Then my sole relief was to . . . allow my mind's eye to dwell on whatever bright visions rose before
it—and certainly they were many and glowing . . . quickened with
all of incident, life, fire, feeling, that I desired and had not in my

actual existence" (*JE*, I, 138). And love, when Jane ultimately finds it at Thornfield, is inextricably bound up with the danger she half-desires—with wildness, hallucination, and blood.

IV   *Selfhood, Reason, and Sexuality*

The center section of the novel, which describes how the force of Jane's love for Rochester draws her more and more into his power, is filled with an ambiguity that arises from Charlotte's ambivalent attitudes toward her heroine's experiences and from the fact that her heroine's internal conflicts mirror her own. On the one hand, like Charlotte, who was determined to win economic success, Jane wishes to succeed in "the busy world" (*JE*, I, 138), to attain independence, to achieve the respect of others by keeping "the law given by God; sanctioned by man" (*JE*, II, 102). But on the other hand, like Charlotte who compulsively dreamed of Angria, Jane is dominated by her private imaginative vision and wishes to turn inward on herself to listen not to the voice of society but to "a tale my imagination created, and narrated continuously." It is this tale, spoken to her "inward ear" (*JE*, I, 138), that enables her to recognize and inspires her to cling to her soul-mate.

Knowing that Rochester is different from her in class, believing that he will marry a woman of his own station, Jane, upon observing him with Blanche and her friends, still asserts, "he is not of their kind. I believe he is of mine;—I am sure he is,—I feel akin to him . . . I have something in my brain and heart, in my blood and nerves, that assimilates me mentally to him" (*JE*, I, 225). And governed by this intuitive knowledge, despite the warnings of her reason, she cherishes the pain which her seemingly hopeless passion excites: "I looked [at Mr. Rochester], and had an acute pleasure in looking,—a precious, yet poignant pleasure; pure gold, with a steely point of agony: a pleasure like what the thirst perishing man might feel who knows the well to which he has crept is poisoned, yet stoops and drinks divine draughts nevertheless" (*JE*, I, 224).

In fact, as this image implies, Jane is in part desirous of the suffering and danger which love entails in her world. She is originally attracted to Rochester because he is "dark, strong, and stern" (*JE*, I, 147). As she knows him more fully, the "something" in his character which made her "fear and shrink" as if she "had been wandering amongst volcanic-looking hills, and had suddenly felt the ground quiver, and seen it gape" continues to fascinate her; and with "throbbing heart," she longs "only to dare—to divine it" (*JE*, I, 242). She is irresistibly attracted to the third story of the Hall, whose "narrow, low, and dim passage, . . . with its two rows of small black doors all shut," she recognizes as being "like a corridor in some Bluebeard's castle." To this hallway, which rings with "distinct, formal, mirthless" (*JE*, I, 135) laughter, she is driven when, in "silent revolt against [her] lot" (*JE*, I, 139), she longs for a "power of vision" (*JE*, I,138); and when Rochester asks her to accompany him to Thornfield's darkened, upper regions, she accepts with half-fearful eagerness:

. . . he held a key in his hand: approaching one of the small, black doors, he put it in the lock; he paused and addressed me again.
"You don't turn sick at the sight of blood?"
"I think I shall not: I have never been tried yet."
I felt a thrill while I answered him; but no coldness, and no faint-ness. . . . I put my fingers into his. "Warm and steady," was his remark; he turned the key and opened the door. (*JE*, I, 269)

The nearly fatal risk entailed in Jane's surrender to the passion which her imagination evokes and sustains is suggested by this movement to the center of the labyrinth. Her "feelings" already "fettered" by his "influence" (*JE*, I, 224), she does not recoil when she is "fastened [by Rochester] into one of [the] mystic cells," separated by a single door from the spot where "mystery" and "crime" live "incarnate." Jane does not wholly understand her peril until she has fully committed herself to her lover; but as she is ineluctably drawn to the total submission he demands, she is increasingly beset by fears. When the month of courtship draws to an end and Jane realizes "there was no putting off the [wedding] day that advanced" (*JE*, II, 46), the being who has been hidden in the secret room breaks from its prison and, like an incubus, comes to stand by the bedside of the sleeping Jane, whose ominous dreams of ruin and death are the product of half-formed fears of the new life she is about to enter upon as Mrs. Rochester.

The subconscious terrors which have haunted Jane since child-hood come to focus on her fear of the conclusion to which her ungoverned passions are leading her. Rochester begins his court-ship with the warning that the emotions he intends to awaken in her will bring her "to a craggy pass of the channel, where the whole of life's stream will be broken up into whirl and tumult, foam and

noise" (*JE*, I, 182). Images of gulfs, abysses, and drowning prolifer-
ate as she struggles to control "feelings" that would "hurry her to
wild chasms" (*JE*, I, 260). As a child, pictures of such scenes filled
her mind with "half-comprehended notions" (*JE*, I, 3); as an adult,
strange "subjects had . . . risen vividly on [her] mind," and she had
"attempted to embody" what she saw "with the spiritual eye" (*JE*, I,
159) in paintings of arctic wastes and of sinking wrecks in storm-
tossed seas. Finally committed to a love which she knows is perfidi-
ous but which she is helpless to extinguish, she feels "the torrent
come": "in full, heavy swing [it] poured over me. . . . 'the waters
came into my soul; I sank in deep mire: I felt no standing; I came
into deep waters; the floods overflowed me' " (*JE*, II, 75).

Jane's first imagined and then realized danger is but one aspect of
Charlotte's own ambivalent attitude toward the consequences of
sexual awakening. Jane finds in Rochester a force which, like the sun
and the fire to which she consistently compares him, warms her into
life. But although she longs to live in the "sunshine of his presence"
(*JE*, II, 8), Rochester's ruthless will, coupled with her own uncontrollable passion, makes him a figure of danger; and while she needs
him and seeks to win him, she fears to be won by him. The
Thornfield garden proposal scene, in which Jane moves from despair to happiness, is riddled with the ambiguities which charac-
terize this section of the novel. Traditionally, gardens are emblematic not only of fruition and peace but also of temptation and betrayal; and the nightingale, whose plaintive song interrupts Rochester's proposal, is the symbol of both romantic love and murderous
lust. In Thornfield's moonlit garden, Rochester ominously calls
Jane's attention to the singing bird as he engages her in a battle of
wills which she loses.

Despite the warnings of "Reason," Jane has "rejected the real,
and rabidly devoured the ideal." Although she knows "it is madness
in all women to let a secret love kindle within them" (*JE*, I, 205),
she has given in to this insanity and, despite her warnings to herself,
has "lavish[ed] the love of the whole heart, soul, and strength,
where [she is forced to believe] such a gift is not wanted and would
be despised" (*JE*, I, 208). Thus she is helpless to defend herself
against her lover's psychological brutality. Her courage and her
sense of her own worth remain intact and lead to the anguished
assertion, "If God had gifted me with some beauty, and much
wealth, I should have made it as hard for you to leave me, as it is

now for me to leave you. . . . it is my spirit that addresses your spirit; just as if both had passed through the grave, and we stood at God's feet, equal,—as we are!" But her vehement self-defense is a confession of her weakness. Thus, Rochester receives proof that he has won: he has forced her to acknowledge her passionate dependence upon him without committing himself; and the significance of his victory is revealed in his vision of Jane as a "wild, frantic bird that is rending its own plumage in its desperation" (*JE*, II, 17–18) and in his gently mocking reminder, "Janet, . . . it was you who made me the offer" (*JE*, II, 30).

Jane fights against Rochester's increasingly possessive will, opposing his desire to "clasp . . . bracelets on [her] wrists," to fasten a "diamond chain round [her] neck," because she is aware that if she accepts these gifts, she will lose her identity: "I shall not be . . . Jane Eyre any longer, but an ape in a harlequin's jacket." Attracted to Jane by his belief that she will serve as an anodyne for his soul's sickness, Rochester is determined to possess her totally and to force her to function as the "angel" and "comforter" he believes her to be. And although she insists, "I am not an angel . . . and I will not be one till I die: I will be myself" (*JE*, II, 25–26), she daily loses more of the power she needs to retain an independent mind and spirit. With her only remaining weapon, the "needle of repartee" (*JE*, II, 44), she skillfully manages to prolong the struggle; but Rochester, who knows her triumphs are small and fleeting, confidently predicts his coming victory: " 'when once I have fairly seized you, to have and to hold, I'll just—figuratively speaking—attach you to a chain like this' (touching his watchguard)" (*JE*, II, 40). Although she hates his complacent satisfaction and bitterly accuses him of wearing a "smile . . . such as a sultan might, in a blissful and fond moment, bestow on a slave his gold and gems had enriched" (*JE*, II, 38), she acknowledges the approaching defeat toward which her own desire drives her: "my task was not an easy one; often I would rather have pleased than teased him. My future husband was becoming to me my whole world" (*JE*, II, 45).

As the day of marriage nears when she will cease to be Jane Eyre and will become "one Jane Rochester, a person whom as yet I knew not" (*JE*, II, 46), her fears of losing her identity increase and are given form and substance by her dreams of ruin, suffering, and loneliness. Her love wars with her fear as she arrays herself "to meet, the dread, but adored, type of my unknown future day" (*JE*,

II, 61); and when—garbed in her wedding dress—she turns toward the mirror, she sees a "veiled figure, so unlike my usual self that it seemed almost the image of a stranger" (*JE*, II, 62).

Jane's response to the disruption of the marriage ceremony is, therefore, as ambivalent as were her anticipatory visions of her wedding. Her initial reaction is a despair so total that she lies "faint; longing to be dead" (*JE*, II, 75); but as Rochester, who had patronized and dominated her, becomes the suppliant and pleads for her love, Jane's sleeping will revives. She has always sought not just respect, but praise; not just equality, but superiority. Pride and a sense of her preeminent merit led Jane to assert to her aunt that far from being inferior to her cousins, "they are not fit to associate with me" (*JE*, I, 29); the same attitude led her to dismiss her rival—the beautiful, well-born Blanche Ingram—as being "a mark beneath jealousy: she was too inferior to excite the feeling" (*JE*, I, 239). This same sense of her own worth at first controlled Jane's response to Rochester; but when she demanded in Thornfield's garden that he see her as his "equal" (*JE*, II, 18), her own overwhelming love for him had itself rendered her inferior and incapable of pressing her claim. Now the situation is reversed, and she sees that she has at least "the passing second of time . . . in which to control and restrain him. . . . I felt an inward power; a sense of influence, which supported me. The crisis was perilous; but not without its charm" (*JE*, II, 83).

The moment will, as Jane clearly sees, decide her destiny. Rochester, who insists that "to live familiarly with inferiors is degrading" and who asserts, "I now hate the recollection of the time I passed with Céline, Giacinta, and Clara," begs Jane to become his mistress since he cannot make her his wife. Jane knows that if she assents to becoming "the successor of these poor girls, he would one day regard me with the same feeling which now in his mind desecrated their memory" (*JE*, II, 95); for during the last weeks as she began "mechanically to obey him" (*JE*, II, 34), she has, like them, become a mere puppet, a doll—a plaything to be cast aside when play is done.

The terms in which she couches her refusal to become his mistress are highly significant: she refuses not out of obedience to "Conscience" or "Reason," for they "turned traitors against me, and charged me with crime in resisting him"; she refuses not because she has ceased to love him, for "feeling" "clamoured wildly," saying,

"Oh, comply" (*JE*, II, 102). Rather, she remains adamant in her rejection of Rochester's plea because of her steadfast belief that in this ultimate crisis her own needs are superior to all other demands, that they justify even her decision to function as "the instrument of evil to what [she] wholly love[s]" (*JE*, II, 109). She thus decides to abandon her lover to what she knows will be "misery" and to what she fears will be "ruin" (*JE*, II, 108) on the grounds that she must obey that "indomitable" inner voice which insists, "*I* care for myself. The more solitary, the more friendless, the more unsustained I am, the more I will respect myself" (*JE*, II, 102). To his anguished cry, "Oh, Jane, this is bitter! This—this is wicked. It would not be wicked to love me," she coldly responds, "It would to obey you" (*JE*, II, 102).

V *Jane Triumphant*

Jane's flight in the middle of the night saves her from psychological destruction, but it does not lead to her happiness and safety. Rather, her panicked flight from the temptation she continues to feel and fear is a negative move that commits her to an existence as perilous as the one she flees. At Moor House, she comes to see how cold repression of all feeling results only in spiritual imprisonment, the end of which is destruction. She finds that under St. John's influence, her mind becomes a "rayless dungeon" (*JE*, II, 217), and she realizes that the man whose "Christianity covers human deformity" (*JE*, II, 180) "could soon kill [her]" (*JE*, II, 229).

Jane's struggle to maintain her independence when she is threatened by St. John's powerful will parallels her battle against Rochester. The two men represent the antithetical forces of passion and reason which exist within Jane; therefore, part of her nature spontaneously responds to each.[4] Jane fully realizes that Rochester and St. John see her differently and wish to wed her for different reasons but that, despite these differences, they both seek to destroy her selfhood. Rochester—who believes her to be innocent and pure—wishes to force her to function as his "better self," his "good angel" (*JE*, II, 99). St. John—who believes she is in danger of becoming a spiritual "castaway" (*JE*, II, 233) and a "vessel of wrath" doomed to "perdition" (*JE*, II, 238)—wishes to save her endangered soul, thus carrying out the directive of Christ his master and, at the same time, winning a "useful tool" (*JE*, II, 235) which he can wield for the glory of God. He informs Jane that in rejecting his proposal, "it is not me you deny, but God. Through my means, He opens to you a noble career; as my wife only can you enter upon it. Refuse to be my wife, and you limit yourself for ever to a track of selfish ease and barren obscurity. Tremble lest in that case you should be numbered with those who have denied the faith and are worse than infidels!" (*JE*, II, 225–26). He will be satisfied with nothing less than her total surrender: as a Christian, he may "patiently" bear her "perversity"; but "as a man, he . . . wished to coerce [her] into obedience" (*JE*, II, 226).

The grounds on which Jane ultimately rejects the demands of St. John are the same as those on which she denied the commands of Rochester: in both cases, she steadfastly asserts that her own needs must take precedence over all other considerations. Clearly, despite her habitual and characterizing use of the conventional language of Christianity, Jane is not motivated by a Christian concern to save her soul by submitting her will to God's. Instead, she uses religion to justify following the self-seeking course to which she is already committed. She rationalizes her decision to leave Rochester by insisting that she must "keep the law given by God; sanctioned by man" (*JE*, II, 102); but when St. John—whose "sternness" is that of "the warrior Great-heart" (*JE*, II, 283)—speaks, she refuses to obey, although at the very moment, "Religion called—Angels beckoned—God commanded" (*JE*, II, 239).

Despite the fact that at this climactic moment, she believes she is deciding the fate of her soul and feels that "for safety and bliss [in eternity], all here might be sacrificed in a second" (*JE*, II, 239), she hesitates to make the sacrifice demanded of her and acts at last only when the answer to her prayer for guidance is the one she wants to hear—the voice of Rochester calling her back to him. Her immediate triumph over St. John's power is stated in terms which confirm Jane's sense of the absolute correctness of her own inner drives and her total confidence in her ability to assert her will:

I broke from St. John. . . . It was *my* time to assume ascendancy. *My* powers were in play, and in force. . . . Where there is energy to command well enough, obedience never fails. I mounted to my chamber; . . . fell on my knees; and prayed in my way—a different way to St. John's, but effective in its own fashion. I seemed to penetrate very near a Mighty Spirit. . . . I rose . . .—took a resolve—and lay down, unscared, enlightened—eager but for the daylight. (*JE*, II, 240–41)

Jane has long fluctuated between the two equally dangerous extremes of "absolute submission and determined revolt" (*JE*, II, 214), but she has now achieved the power to command herself and others continually and forcefully; and her decision to return to Thornfield, where, as far as she knows, nothing has changed, reveals her confidence in her ability to live in her "unscared, enlightened" state. Having learned that "energy" commands "obedience" (*JE*, II, 241), Jane will be ruthless if she must; and rather than bend to another's will, she will, if necessary, break her opponent. There is an element of cruelty in Jane's first meeting with the maimed Rochester. Rochester's victory in the battle of wills which occurred at Thornfield is balanced by Jane's victory in the similar battle at Ferndean: as Rochester used Blanche Ingram to force Jane into an impassioned admittance of dependence, so Jane uses St. John Rivers as a pawn in a replay of that former, cruel struggle; and Jane's previous agonized admission to her lover that she sees her dismissal "in the shape of Miss Ingram; a noble and beautiful woman,—your bride" (*JE*, II, 17), is echoed in Rochester's bitter recognition of his defeat: "Go. . . . Your own way—with the husband you have chosen. . . . this St. John Rivers" (*JE*, II, 272).

The completeness of Jane's victory appears when she, who has so often been thought of as a caged or injured bird which "quiver[s] its shattered pinions" (*JE*, II, 112) and "rend[s] its own plumage" (*JE*, II, 18), now becomes a "sky-lark" (*JE*, II, 266); and Rochester is reduced to a "fettered wild beast or bird," a "caged eagle" (*JE*, II, 256). Although Jane has become an independent woman, hers is a perverse victory: in a world which allows her no hope of absolute contentment, in which struggle is inevitable and unending, she can succeed finally only by using the brutal control she demonstrates as she bends at last over the "shaggy black mane" (*JE*, II, 264) of her "sightless Samson" (*JE*, II, 256).

The conclusion of the novel thus chronicles the totality of Jane's triumph over all that has threatened and opposed her will—society, St. John, Rochester, religion—and illuminates the gravity of the decision she has made. The last words of *Jane Eyre* are devoted not to Rochester and to Jane's domestic bliss, but to a summary of St. John's career as a "high master-spirit, which aims to fill a place in the first rank of those who are redeemed from the earth . . . who are called, and chosen, and faithful" (*JE*, II, 283–84). At the crisis of her relationship with St. John, Jane refuses this call to service and redemption. "I contended with my inward dimness of vision" (*JE*, II, 239), she remarks; and she responds only when her entreaty for direction is answered by the illumination of her titular feminine deity, the moon,[5] which directs her not toward the pilgrim way of St. John, leading to the "throne of God," but back into the world. St. John "entered on the path" to eternal life, obeying "the exaction of the apostle, who speaks but for Christ, when he says— 'Whosoever will come after me, let him deny himself, and take up his cross and follow me' " (*JE*, II, 283).

When St. John proposes, Jane experiences a sensation "as if I had heard a summons from Heaven," but she insists, "I was no apostle,—I could not behold the herald,—I could not receive his call" (*JE*, II, 216); instead, she responds to the "voice of a human being—a known, loved, well-remembered voice" which, significantly enough, calls only her name, "nothing more" (*JE*, II, 240); and although at the time of her decision not to marry St. John, she for a moment saw "death's gates opening, . . . eternity beyond" (*JE*, II, 239), she returns to the labyrinth of physical experience. Seeking her lover, she enters the "gloomy wood" of Ferndean and walks along "a grass-grown track . . . between hoar and knotty shafts and under branched arches": "I thought I had taken a wrong direction and lost my way. The darkness of natural as well as of sylvan dusk gathered over me: I looked round in search of another road. There was none: all was interwoven stem, columnar trunk, dense, summer foliage—no opening anywhere" (*JE*, II, 254–55).

But at the center of the maze is her goal: "a figure came out into the twilight. . . . I had recognized him—it was my master, Edward Fairfax Rochester, and no other" (*JE*, II, 255). The closing words of the novel are St. John Rivers': "My master . . . has forewarned me. Daily he announces more distinctly,—'Surely I come quickly!' and hourly I more eagerly respond,—'Amen; even so come, Lord Jesus' " (*JE*, II, 284); but Jane waits for no heavenly fulfillment—her apotheosis is achieved on her own terms and in this world.

Almost from the day of its first publication, readers have argued over the nature of the morality and the quality of the religious thought in *Jane Eyre*. Charlotte acknowledged herself "distressed" by a contemporary review which insisted that Jane "is the personification of an unregenerate and undisciplined spirit" and that her strength "is the strength of a mere heathen mind which is a law unto itself."[6] Yet a close reading of the novel seems to support this view.

Given the fact that ultimately and triumphantly Jane achieves not only what her own spirit demands but what her maimed lover comes to desire, it is difficult to believe that Charlotte, with her extensive knowledge of Christian doctrine[7] and her familiarity with both Milton and the Bible, was unaware that the situation in which she finally placed her heroine not only celebrates Jane's decision to be governed solely by her own will but reverses the traditional Christian view of the superiority of men over women.

The perverse echo of *Paradise Lost* is explicit: Eve entered upon her temptation doomed to fall by her insistence on independence from Adam, her "best Prop," but the blind and maimed Rochester leans upon Jane, who has become "both his prop and guide" (*JE*, II, 278). Jane has always insisted on being the center of her own world; she is now also the center of Rochester's. God has been removed from his throne, and Jane reigns supreme. The chastened Rochester whom Jane finds at Ferndean insists he has acknowledged the existence of supernatural power, has repented his past life, and has sought to reform himself in accordance with Christian principles; but in truth, Rochester worships only Jane—he has "supplicated God, that if it seemed good to Him, I might soon be taken from this life, and admitted to that world to come, where there was still hope of rejoining Jane" (*JE*, II, 276); and his only verbalized prayer is limited to the single word which is "the alpha and omega of [his] heart's wishes": "Jane! Jane! Jane!" (*JE*, II, 277). Hearing him speak of this invocation which calls her back, Jane implicitly equates herself with the Virgin Mary, saying, "I kept these things then, and pondered them in my heart" (*JE*, II, 278). So Jane remains consistent to the end: her "sweetest wishes" (*JE*, II, 282), which have been so totally fulfilled, are, as the condition of her world demands, selfish wishes.

At the end of this novel, there is no attempt as in Jane Austen's *Pride and Prejudice* (1813) to establish a sanctuary for those who are worthy, and no decision as in George Eliot's *Middlemarch* (1871–1872) to go out into the world to serve. Instead, Jane and Rochester retreat into a private world in which Jane is superior and, therefore, satisfied.

A critical evaluation of *Jane Eyre* is in one sense made unnecessary, if not presumptuous, by the fact that generations of readers have established Jane as one of the characters of English literature who have attained virtually mythic proportions. Charlotte Brontë's story of a plain orphan girl whose superior qualities are finally acknowledged and who gains the reward of love and power has become the modern version of the Cinderella tale; for Jane not only wins her Prince Charming but does so by steadfastly asserting her independence, becoming thereby not merely his consort but his queen.

To give new meaning and new life to a myth is in itself a major achievement, but in *Jane Eyre*, Charlotte does more. Not simply a symbol, Jane is a fully realized psychological entity whose nature is delineated both through conversation and monologue, and through surreal setting and atmosphere. The trackless, barren heath surrounding Moor House and the "storm-beat" lawn of Gateshead are emblematic of Jane's internal state; Thornfield with its hidden, raving inmate is both a complex symbol for the dangerous passions within Jane, and a microcosm of the threatening universe she postulates.

The unrealistic and melodramatic details of the plot are submerged in the compelling surge of Jane's first-person narration. Clearly, the world Jane sees is that which *her* eyes create: we are concerned while reading her story not with what is, but with what she believes to be true. Totally self-involved, Jane sees others only as adjuncts or impediments to her own fulfillment. Her depiction of the Reeds and the members of the Thornfield house party as one-dimensional characters given to unmotivated cruelty, expresses a truth beyond slice-of-life realism; for to her exacerbated sensibility, their refusal to facilitate her happiness is villainous. Similarly, her absorption in the self which makes of the exterior world a symbolic system that reflects and directs her progress to her goals, allows the reader to accept, as Jane does, the seeming intervention of the supernatural in the form of storm, dream, vision, and telepathic communication.

In *Jane Eyre*, Charlotte found a means of universalizing the imaginative vision of Angria. Split between the wish to remain safely passive and the need to indulge in the excitement of rebellion; approving the severely rational, yet delighting and trusting in intuition, imagination, and vision; desiring sexual satisfaction, yet fearing passion—Jane is not only a fictionalized version of her creator but the very epitome of modern mankind, who, having chosen to turn inward for authority, finds only ambivalence and confusion. In her struggles to wrest safety, comfort, and love from her hostile environment, Jane encounters the dangers of our nightmares; in her success, she realizes our dreams.

CHAPTER 5

Shirley

I *The Plot*

SET in 1812, *Shirley* (1849) opens with a description of violence in the industrial north of England. Robert Gèrard Moore has recently come from Antwerp to Yorkshire, the home of his father, and has rented a fabric mill. Like most other cloth manufacturers, Robert is forced to the verge of bankruptcy by the Napoleonic Wars which have destroyed the international market. To increase production and to reduce overhead, Robert has followed the lead of his competitors and has bought new machinery which, by mechanizing his operation, has thrown many of his employees out of work. Frightened by the prospect of being driven from their homes and forced to live in abject poverty, the workers have begun to fight back against their employers by breaking the machinery which is replacing them. Mr. Helstone, the parish priest, who is motivated both by a militant nature which delights in a good fight and by the Tory belief that property is sacrosanct, sends his curate, Mr. Malone, to Robert's aid and promises to come himself to the mill at the first sign of trouble. But the disaffected mill hands do not wait to attack the mill; instead, they smash the machinery on the road. Robert, like Helstone, feels invigorated by the challenge offered and responds defiantly by promising to import more machinery and to defend it with force. He vows never to give up protecting his threatened property.

Despite love and admiration for Robert, Caroline Helstone—the Reverend Helstone's niece and the daughter of the half-sister of Robert's father—is not blind to the hardness in his nature. She attempts to make him understand that his economic policies are the cause of great pain to others and that by driving other men to desperation, he places himself in peril; but he refuses to change his

106

plans, which he justifies on the grounds of economic necessity. The same awareness of economic necessity makes him repress his growing affection for the portionless Caroline, who at eighteen, finds herself trapped in a sterile life. She has no meaningful duties to perform in her uncle's home, and the mere fact she is a woman keeps her from entering business and making her own way in the world. Her woman-hating uncle, who after her father's death took her in out of a sense of duty but cares nothing for her and understands nothing of her nature and her needs, refuses to let her accept the only sort of job for which she is qualified—that of a governess. With nothing else to think of, she dwells against her will on her unrequited love for Robert; and although she urges herself to be stoic in her suffering, she succumbs to greater and greater depression.

Meanwhile, Shirley Keeldar, the young heiress to the estate of which Moore's mill is a part, arrives with Mrs. Pryor—once her governess and now her companion—to take up residence at the great house, Fieldhead. Orphaned early in life, Shirley is blessed with great beauty, wealth, and intelligence; but these qualities, which bring her the respect and admiration of all, have unfitted her to play the traditional submissive female role. Now of age and independent, Shirley enters with high spirits and great energy into parish affairs, including the dispute between employees and employers. Attracted by Caroline's good sense and good nature, she becomes closely attached to the lonely girl, who, for a time, is invigorated by this new and longed-for companionship.

Adamant in his purpose, Robert Moore again buys machinery; and this time, having fortified his mill and engaged the services of men who share his economic beliefs, he defends his property against a band of armed rioters. He wins a momentary victory, but he lives in greater danger than ever from the anger of the defeated and desperate workers.

Caroline, who believes that Robert wishes to marry Shirley and who has witnessed Shirley's admiration of and eagerness to aid him in his spirited defense, now falls ill. Bereft of all hope that Robert will ever return her love and believing that no one cares deeply for her, she daily slips closer to death, although for a time her very declaration that nothing is seriously wrong disguises the gravity of her case from the casual observation of those about her. Only Mrs. Pryor, who has long expressed great fondness for Caroline, discerns the girl's true condition; and she is helpless to arrest the seemingly inexorable decline. Perceiving that it is grief which is fatally sapping Caroline's will to live, Mrs. Pryor, who has come to nurse her, discovers that her patient is hopelessly in love with Robert; and unable to offer any comfort for this pain, yet desperate to give Caroline reason to live, she reveals to the girl that she is her mother. Years before, Mrs. Pryor's fear of her husband had driven her from him and their child; believing her daughter happy and fearing to risk loving again, she had refused to disclose her identity to Caroline until the fear that she would lose her forever drove her to speak. Caroline, who for years has wondered about her mother and has taken her parents' desertion as evidence that she lacks the qualities that will call forth love, is given new life by this announcement; and she begins to recover.

Her health regained, Caroline finds Shirley engaged in a battle of wills with her Uncle Sympson. He, his wife, his son, and his son's tutor, Louis Moore, who is Robert's brother, have come to visit Fieldhead; and he is busy urging his recalcitrant niece to accept a rich young man as her husband. Shirley, who refuses on the grounds that she neither likes nor respects the gentleman in question, seems little disturbed by her uncle's anger. But at length, she shows signs of distress so severe that her young cousin, who finds she has recently made her will, becomes afraid and goes to Louis Moore with the news that Shirley believes she will soon die.

Louis questions Shirley, who pledges him to obey her commands and keep her secret, and then announces that she fears she has been infected by hydrophobia. Although she has cauterized the wound by placing a red-hot Italian iron on her arm, she mistrusts the effectiveness of this treatment and forces Louis to promise that if she does go mad, he will protect her from all attempts to treat her and will himself administer so strong a dose of narcotic as to "leave no mistake." Shirley's fears are soon proved groundless, but her firmness of mind in this crisis increases Louis' love for this girl who was once his pupil but whose wealth and social position have kept him from approaching as a lover.

The frustration and fury of the mill workers continues to increase, and one night a weaver, in a frenzy induced by religious fervor and drink, shoots Robert Moore. As he lies near death, Robert revaluates his life and comes to despise what now seems to him his mad decision to sacrifice all to his pride and his desire for economic success. He acknowledges his love for Caroline and asks her to marry him; and she, made confident and happy by her mother's love and now more capable of displaying her feelings, accepts him gladly.

Louis Moore now prepares to depart from Fieldhead with Shirley's uncle, for he believes that the social distance between himself and Shirley is an insurmountable barrier to marriage. However, as the time of parting nears, Louis' passion forces him to speak, to cast aside social conventions, and to force Shirley to admit that she loves him. Shirley accepts his proposal even though her feelings are ambivalent: she hates and fears the loss of independence which she knows will be the consequence of her marriage to Louis, whom she loves partly because he is determined to control her. The end of the war relieves the acute social tensions in the parish, and the two marriages are solemnized amid the victory celebrations.

II   *The Social Milieu*

Shirley is broader in scope than Charlotte's other novels, for it directs the reader's attention to two heroines and sets their stories against a background of economic, social, and religious strife. Ostensibly, *Shirley* is an historical novel set in Yorkshire, where in 1812, the industrial revolution, coupled with the Napoleonic Wars, produced riots which seemed to be the forerunner of violent political and class warfare. Charlotte had heard many stories of these days told by people who had witnessed the desperate mill workers smashing the new cloth manufacturing machinery which threatened their livelihood. Undoubtedly influenced by the literary fashion of the time for novels of social significance,[1] Charlotte chose a subject which allowed her to call attention to the insolvable problems inherent in an inevitable social change which initially disrupts old social and economic structures without providing new ones into which individuals can fit themselves. Trapped by grinding economic necessity but unable to derive any useful knowledge from the past or to discern the end to which forces that control them are inexorably moving, master and man, in their desperate effort to preserve themselves, break the economic bond which once offered mutual self-benefit and become murderous opponents in a struggle that can lead only to defeat for both sides.

But Charlotte uses the Yorkshire machine breaking just as she earlier used the Angrian wars—not as a subject in itself but as background material to help establish an atmosphere of brutality and frustration and to help define the problem of the individual who finds himself victimized by a corrupt and inimical society. Although she recognizes that men as well as women exist in jeopardy, she directs attention more fully to women, who are shown as victimized not only by inexorable political and economic forces but also by men, who are far from omnipotent individually but who collectively hold the reins of social power.

Before beginning *Shirley*, Charlotte wrote to Mr. Williams, of Smith, Elder and Company, saying, "I often wish to say something about the 'condition of women' question."[2] Her own experiences qualified her to speak of the day-to-day frustrations and sufferings that were the lot of poor but intelligent and sensitive girls; watching her talented sisters slowly die virtually unknown and unpraised as she struggled to complete this novel increased her bitterness. Indeed, it is widely assumed that with their deaths, Charlotte altered her manuscript by turning Caroline Helstone and Shirley Keeldar into idealized representations of Anne and Emily.[3] *Shirley*, however, does more than memorialize the two beings Charlotte loved most: it presents Caroline and Shirley as martyrs to perverse social and religious doctrines. The novel is a bitter polemic which fully reveals the inferior status of women, the injustices consistently practiced upon them, and their consequent misery. Deprived of power and totally unable to reform or even to alter the tyrannical system under which they suffer, these women are also betrayed by their own natures, which turn traitor against them and urge them into destructive conformity.

Charlotte describes with great care the perverse, vicious, and chaotic nature of the society in which men and women work out their destinies. As the book opens, the utter disorder of the international and national scene has so undermined the economic basis of the community that the entire social structure is threatened with collapse:

The "Orders in Council," provoked by Napoleon's Milan and Berlin decrees, and forbidding neutral powers to trade with France, had, by offending America, cut off the principal market of the Yorkshire woollen trade, and brought it consequently to the verge of ruin. Minor foreign markets were glutted, and would receive no more: the Brazils, Portugal, Sicily, were all overstocked by nearly two years' consumption. At this crisis, certain inventions in machinery were introduced into the staple manufactures of the north, which, greatly reducing the number of hands necessary to be employed, threw thousands out of work, and left them without legitimate means of sustaining life. A bad harvest supervened. Distress reached its climax. Endurance, over-goaded, stretched the hand of fraternity to sedition.[4]

The society thus stricken is innately corrupt. Having placed its faith in material values, starved the affections, and ignored the soul, the citizenry lacks the means and the will to control the fear which sweeps over it when the system it has willingly perpetuated begins to break down: "National honour has become a mere empty name of no value in the eyes of many, because their sight was dim with famine; and for a morsel of meat they would have sold their birthright. . . . The throes of a sort of moral earthquake were felt heaving under the hills of the northern countries" (*S*, I, 29–30).

Driven by the instinct for self-preservation, both the men who seek to break the machines and those who are determined to defend them are mutually uninhibited in pursuing their ends, for they are members of a society where compassion and forgiveness are almost unknown and where an injury once received is never forgotten: "the people of this country bear malice: it is the boast of some of them that they can keep a stone in their pocket seven years, turn it at the end of that time, keep it seven years longer, and hurl it, and hit their mark 'at last' " (*S*, I, 134). In this world, religion no longer instills the principles of charity and humility in the hearts of men, but has become the source of internecine conflict; in fact, theological differences are used both to foment and justify strife. The dissenters use anticlericalism to urge the poor to rebel against their employers; and the members of the establishment—led by the "clerical Cossack" Helstone, who "should have been a soldier, [although] circumstances had made him a priest" (*S*, I, 37), and by curates who quarrel "whenever they meet" (*S*, I, 3)—employ the doctrine of a God-created hierarchical system to justify a conservative political stance.

Charlotte uses this economic crisis to convey that man is inevitably confronted by acute, unresolvable dilemmas which inspire panic and desperate acts, even though such acts are useless or self-destructive. In describing the interaction of Robert Moore, the manufacturer; Shirley Keeldar, his landlord; William Farren, an unemployed worker; and Moses Barraclough, the Methodist leader of frightened and hungry mill workers, Charlotte delineates the complexity of the crisis facing them all. Despite innate differences in character and radically opposed political, economic, and religious philosophies, each is inexorably driven toward a confrontation with the others which will resolve nothing and can only increase the pain and suffering they already experience.

Robert, who has sought to obey the injunction of his society to achieve economic success and who has come to England to rebuild his fortunes by following the family trade of cloth manufacturing, finds himself the victim of an international situation which threatens to throw him into bankruptcy and thus prevent him from contributing to the economic support of others, despite his willingness to do so. But Robert will not give up: although he has no assurance that the installation of machinery will save him from economic disaster, he realizes his only hope of survival lies in using machinery to reduce his overhead. Compelled by the irresistible force of economic change as much as by his pride, which refuses to accept defeat, he determines to industrialize his mill despite the pleas and the anger of men this course of action will put out of work: "If I did as you wish me to do, I should be bankrupt in a month: and would my bankruptcy put bread into your hungry children's mouths? William Farren, neither to your dictation, nor to that of any other, will I submit. Talk to me no more about machinery; I will have my own way. I shall get new frames in to-morrow:—If you broke these, I would still get more. *I'll never give in*" (S, I, 151).

But the workers, made desperate by their own and their families' suffering, are like Robert, the victims of forces beyond their control. William Farren, who no less than Robert has lived by the long-established rules of his society, working hard and honestly in exchange for his wages, now finds that the system he has believed in has betrayed him; thus, he is forced to alter both his convictions and his actions: "I'm getting different to mysel': I feel I am changing. I wad n't heed, if t' bairns and t' wife had enough to live on; but they're pinched—they're pined—" (S, I, 154). Beyond the control of either worker or employer, the situation has no solution. Robert states the truth when he insists to Barraclough, the rabble-rouser, that the physical violence he threatens is, at best, a short-term solution:

You desire me to quit the country; you request me to part with my machinery; in case I refuse, you threaten me. I *do* refuse—point-blank! Here I stay; and by this mill I stand; and into it will I convey the best machinery inventors can furnish. What will you do? The utmost you *can* do—and this you will never *dare* to do—is to burn down my mill, destroy its contents, and shoot me. What then? Suppose that building was a ruin and I was a corpse, what then?—you lads behind these two scamps, would that stop invention or exhaust science?—Not for the fraction of a second of time! Another and better gig-mill would rise on the ruins of this, and perhaps a more enterprising owner come in my place. (*S*, I, 149)

Farren, unable to answer, can perceive the injustice of the situation; and he insists that "invention may be all right, but I know it is n't right for poor folks to starve. Them tha governs mun find a way to help us." But those who "govern" are, as they see, themselves victims: urged by William to make his "changes rather more slowly," Robert asserts bitterly, "if I stopped by the way an instant, while others are rushing on, I should be trodden down" (*S*, I, 151).

III *The Inferior Position of Women: Cause and Consequence*

Charlotte closely links economic warfare and the battle of the sexes which rages within this society.[5] Men and women, like employer and employee, are locked in a vicious and useless struggle. Hating and fearing their own sexuality and that of others, to which they instinctively respond, both men and women assume defensive positions which, since they inhibit their natural desires, are ultimately self-destructive. But although she sees both males and females as victims of corrupt social patterns, Charlotte concentrates on the inferior status of women in a system which men have created and continue to maintain, although they, too, are harmed by it.

The novel elaborates fully upon the fact, the causes, and the consequences of male domination of the female. It is in the economic sphere that the discrimination against women is most apparent; for the society of which they are members, although it places material values above all others, provides them with no means of earning money. A young man has the opportunity "of learning a business, and making [his] way in life" (*S*, I, 76); but a young woman can make money only by becoming either a household servant or a governess. In this latter position, which is the only one open to girls of good family, she slaves for a pittance; is "ever . . . kept in a sort of [social] isolation" (*S*, II, 65); and after "contend[ing] a while courageously with [her] doom" (*S*, II, 67), is broken in health and spirit. Women are, therefore, forced to choose marriage. But if marriage is more necessary for the woman than for the man, it is also infinitely more difficult for her to attain: "A lover masculine . . . disappointed can speak and urge explanation; a lover feminine can say nothing; if she did the result would be shame and anguish, inward remorse for self-treachery" (S, I, 114). And men exult in their tyranny: "The gentlemen turn [women] into ridicule; they don't want them; they hold them very cheap: they say— I have heard them say it with sneering laughs many a time—the matrimonial market is overstocked" (S, II, 82–83).

The image is both ominous and apt; for as it implies, a woman's fate is determined by the economic system in which she has no power, because her desirability as a mate is dependent not on innate qualities but on a monetary worth that she is powerless to increase. The statements of the loutish curate, Malone, which open the discussion of marriage, summarize the views of his society: "If there is one notion I hate more than another, it is that of marriage: I mean marriage in the vulgar weak sense, as a mere matter of sentiment; two beggarly fools agreeing to unite their indigence by some fantastic tie of feeling—humbug! But an advantageous connexion, such as can be formed in consonance with dignity of views, and permanency of solid interests, is not so bad—eh?" (S, I, 22). When Robert Moore confides his desperate financial situation to Mr. Yorke, this respected man of the community offers an easy solution: "if I were circumstanced as you are [,] I should think I could very likely get a wife with a few thousands, who would both suit me and my affairs" (S, I, 181). And Robert takes this advice: he proposes to the heiress Shirley Keeldar, not because he loves her but because he wants "fortune's splendid prize" (S, II, 235).

But if being sold on the marriage market saves a woman from the life of social disrespect and boredom which is the inevitable lot of the old maid, it also is virtually certain to subject her to a life of bondage. For on the authority of the Pauline doctrine that God intends women to be restricted to a position of subservience in all matters, this society assumes that women should function only as the slaves and servants or, at best, as the mindless dependents of their husbands. Indeed, the belief in the innate superiority of men is so strong that it abrogates even the belief in class hierarchy; consequently, Joe Scott, a poorly educated employee of Robert Moore, feels he is qualified to sermonize to both Shirley, his employer's female landlord, and Caroline, the niece of the parish priest. When Shirley asks Scott, "Do you seriously think all the wisdom in the world is lodged in male skulls?" he responds, "I've a great respect for the doctrines delivered in the second chapter of St. Paul's first Epistle to Timothy. . . . Let the woman learn in silence, with all subjection. I suffer not a woman to teach, nor to usurp authority over the man; but to be in silence. For Adam was first formed, then Eve. . . . Adam was not deceived; but the woman, being deceived, was in the transgression." And when Shirley urges that the traditional Protestant doctrine of "the Right of private judgment" in matters of religion be extended to women, Scott denies it totally, saying, "Nay: women is to take their husbands' opinion, both in politics and religion: it's wholesomest for them" (*S*, II, 12–13). The ultimate condition of women is summed up by the bitter Caroline Helstone: married or unmarried, they are condemned to "stay at home" and to "sew and cook." Men "expect them to do this, and this only, contentedly, regularly, uncomplainingly all their lives long, as if they had no germs of faculties for anything else" (*S*, II, 83).

When a man demands that women submit to this social and mental bondage, he also forces them into total psychological dependency while he remains independent. Caroline, who has fallen deeply in love with Robert Moore and who, given no encouragement by him, is compelled to suffer in silence, insists that her situation is exacerbated by the fact that she has nothing to think of *but* her hopeless passion. Although she "long[s] to have something absorbing and compulsory to fill her head and hands, and to occupy her thoughts" (*S*, I, 250), her society denies her such relief and thereby nails her more firmly to her cross: ". . . men and women are so different: they are in such a different position. Women have so few things to think about—men so many: you may have a friendship for a man, while he is almost indifferent to you. Much of what cheers your life may be dependent on him, while not a feeling or interest of moment in his eyes may have reference to you" (*S*, I, 249).

Driven to despair by the belief that she "shall not be married," Caroline asks, "What was I created for . . . ? Where is my place in the world?" She perceives that "certain sets of human beings are very apt to maintain that other sets should give up their lives to them and their service, and then they requite them by praise: they call them devoted and virtuous. Is this enough? Is it to live? Is there not a terrible hollowness, mockery, want, craving, in that existence

which is given away to others, for want of something of your own to
bestow it on? I suspect there is. Does virtue lie in abnegation of
self?" (*S*, I, 193–99).

To this last question, Caroline's society insists that women give an
affirmative answer. As a result, because she is unable to perform
meaningful labor which, while it cannot make a human being happy,
"can give varieties of pain, and prevent [her] from breaking [her]
heart with a single tyrant master-torture" (*S*, I, 250), Caroline is
condemned to "waste [her] youth in aching langour" (*S*, I, 204): "her
memory kept harping on the name of Robert Moore: an elegy over
the past still rung constantly in her ear; a funereal inward cry
haunted and harassed her: the heaviness of a broken spirit, and of
pining and palsying faculties, settled slow on her buoyant youth.
Winter seemed conquering her spring: the mind's soil and its treasures were freezing gradually to barren stagnation" (*S*, I, 205).

Trained by their society to "look forward to marriage with some
one they love as the brightest,—the only bright destiny that can
await them" (*S*, II, 67), women are unable to bear the frequent
subsequent discovery that they have been betrayed by their own
emotions and have given to their husbands what they neither need
nor want. For these women, love "is very bitter. It is said to be
strong—strong as death! Most of the cheats of existence are strong.
As to their sweetness—nothing is so transitory: its date is a
moment,—the twinkling of an eye: the sting remains for ever: it may
perish with the dawn of eternity, but it tortures through time into its
deepest night" (*S*, II, 68).

Throughout *Shirley,* Charlotte suggests that although men insist
that their desire to obey Bible doctrine impels them to limit and
restrict women, men are in truth motivated by a deep and innate
dread of the female sex. The summary of Reverend Helstone's attitude demonstrates that the male's pleasure in watching women
conform to the roles society forces them to play is based on his fear
that they may be naturally capable of far different responses: "At
heart, he could not abide sense in women: he liked to see them as
silly, as light-headed, as vain, as open to ridicule as possible; because they were then in reality what he held them to be, and wished
them to be,—inferior: toys to play with, to amuse a vacant hour and
to be thrown away" (*S*, I, 127). The male's fear of women is also
implied in Shirley Keeldar's comment: "If men could see us as we
really are, they would be a little amazed; but the cleverest, the

acutest men are often under an illusion about women; they do not read them in a true light: they misapprehend them, both for good and evil: their good woman is a queer thing, half doll, half angel; their bad woman almost always a fiend" (*S*, II, 37).

What men find most diabolical in woman is her sexuality which, by inflaming their natural desires, tempts them to abandon the materialistic goals of the value system they have created and to which they have committed themselves. Accordingly, Robert Moore defines his tentative courtship of the penniless Caroline Helstone as a "frenzy" which is evidence of present "weakness" and future "downright ruin" (*S*, I, 104). It is because of this fear of the woman's allure that the man attempts to assign her nonthreatening roles which allow him to ignore or possibly to eliminate her sexual appeal. As long as she can be thought of as a doll—a toy—her sexual attractiveness poses no danger but simply adds to her owner's pleasure in amusing himself with her. Thought of as an angel, she is equally unthreatening because the term, by definition, implies a lack of interest in, and a superiority to, all physical desire.

In *Shirley*, Charlotte examines in some detail the male attempt not only to deny the existence of female sexual response but also to equate purity in the woman with physical weakness and ultimately with death. Because any self-motivated action implies the existence of independent will and because such independence in the woman is thought to be unnatural and sinful, the ideal feminine response is conceived of as that which is most totally passive. And because the ultimate passivity is that of death, dying makes a woman wholly attractive, and death constitutes an apotheosis.

This link between purity and death is explored in the story of Mary Cave, "a girl with the face of a Madonna; a girl of living marble; stillness personified" (*S*, I, 54). Having won her, Helstone, who is convinced "women were a very inferior order of existence" (*S*, I, 55), fails to notice that Mary's innate unresponsiveness has become the lassitude induced by fatal illness; and her subsequent death means little to him since it only intensifies and confirms those qualities which originally attracted him to her. He originally fancied her because "she was beautiful as a monumental angel" (*S*, I, 54), but "*his* wife, after a year or two, was of no great importance to him in any shape, and when she one day, as he thought, suddenly—for he had scarcely noticed her decline— . . . took her leave of him and of life, and there was only a still beautiful-featured mould of clay left, cold and white, in the conjugal couch, he felt his bereavement—who shall say how little?" (S, I, 55).

For Mr. Yorke, another of her suitors, death endows Mary with the qualities for which he continues to love her: enshrined in his recollection as "a peaceful angel" (S, II, 242), she is more satisfactory in death than in life; for as he is finally driven to admit, if she had abandoned her saintly passivity and responded to his love, "the odds are, I should have left her!" (S, II, 244).

Shirley recognizes the male's primordial terror of women who actively use their sexual power. Speaking to Caroline of the siren, one of the traditional representations of woman as a sexually avid demon, Shirley describes this mythological being as "Temptress-terror! monstrous likeness of ourselves," and asserts that "there are men who ascribe to 'woman,' in general such attributes" (S, I, 269). But Charlotte reveals that in their desperation to protect themselves from such temptresses by forcing women into social, mental, and psychological bondage, the male rulers of society create the very monsters they fear. Taught that they must marry, women "scheme, . . . plot, . . . dress to ensnare husbands" (S, II, 82), and are driven "to strive, by scarce modest coquetry and debasing artifice, to gain that position and consideration by marriage, which to celibacy is denied" (S, II, 84).

Far from conferring purity on women, the restrictions placed on them by society may drive them to a perverse aggressiveness which is masked by the appearance of conformity to the role of subservient obedience. Mrs. Yorke, an ardent supporter of the doctrine that the best wife is the best servant to her husband, is a monster. Physically powerful, capable of much, she can find no outlet for her talents except through her role of wife and mother; consequently, she desperately clings to and capitalizes on those few powers available to her by becoming violently possessive of her husband and her children: "She was a very good wife, a very careful mother, looked after her children unceasingly, was sincerely attached to her husband; only, the worst of it was, if she could have had her will, she would not have permitted him to have any friend in the world beside herself: all his relations were insupportable to her, and she kept them at arm's length" (S, I, 162); "the youngest [child] is a baby on the mother's knee; it is all her own yet—and that one she has not yet begun to doubt, suspect, condemn; it derives its sustenance from her, it hangs on her, it clings to her, it loves her above everything else in the world: she is sure of that, because, as it lives by her, it cannot be otherwise, therefore she loves it" (*S*, I, 163). Desiring power but having only one area in which to seek it, she aggressively aggrandizes the little authority she gains and savagely turns on any who dare to oppose her. The irony that is implicit in the character of this dictatorial matriarch, who is "as much disposed to gore as any vicious 'mother of the herd' " (*S*, II, 96), is plain; to have power in this society, the woman must conform to the limited role of house-keeper and bearer of children; and the society which requires such conformity not only creates but ultimately applauds as virtuous the man-eating, child-devouring female monster of myth.

Although *Shirley* makes clear Charlotte's assumption that woman's inferior social position is destructive of herself and of others, she also admits that some women are so weak, perverse, or stupid that they willingly accept the role men wish them to play. In fact, her view of the condition of women is so black that she concedes that such women as Hannah Sykes who "demanded no respect; only flattery: if her admirers only *told* her that she was an angel, she would let them *treat* her like an idiot" (*SE*, I, 127–28), are perhaps the most fortunate: "It is good for women, especially, to be endowed with a soft blindness: to have mild, dim eyes, that never penetrate below the surface of things—that take all for what it seems: thousands, knowing this, keep their eyelids drooped, on system" (*S*, I, 300).

IV   *Caroline Helstone's Story*

Caroline Helstone and Shirley Keeldar—to their despair—are not blind to the horror of their situation; and the stories of these women—one by nature a passive sufferer; the other, a natural rebel—fully illuminate the pain born of knowledge of what their society and their natures condemn them to. The story of Caroline Helstone is a study of the consequences of defeat and hopelessness. By nature warm and loving, she has lived from childhood with her cold, authoritarian uncle, Reverend Helstone, who despises women as inferior beings and who lacks both the capacity and the desire to offer love to his niece. Although "conscientious" and "faithful," he is "a man almost without sympathy, ungentle, prejudiced, and rigid" (*S*, I, 37). Knowing that as an infant she was abandoned by her

mother and remembering that her father "was not a good man, and
that he was never kind to her" (S, I, 111), Caroline grows up with a
sense of her own worthlessness.

When the novel opens, she is described as "usually most tranquil,
too dejected and thoughtful indeed sometimes" (S, I, 72); but under
her placid exterior there is a flame which threatens to consume her
utterly. She infinitely prefers the sweet romanticism of Chénier's
"La Jeune Captive" to the classicism of Racine and Corneille, and
the "incoherent comments" she utters when she finishes a fervid
recitation of the poem lead her severe cousin Hortense to exclaim
that there are "glimpses of unsettled hurry in her nature" (S, I,
72–73). Caroline is discontented with her life, and she at times
despises her femininity, which condemns her to a dull servitude: "I
should like an occupation; and if I were a boy, it would not be so
difficult to find one" (S, I, 76).

Her greatest desire, however, is to be loved as she loves, and she
focuses her hopes on her cousin Robert Moore; but both the attitudes of her society and Robert's character present obstacles which
she cannot effectively overcome. She is a woman and, therefore,
cannot speak first; she must be chosen but cannot herself choose;
and although she is convinced of the rightness of her feelings, she
can take no action to achieve what she so actively desires: "Now, I
love Robert, and I feel sure that Robert loves me. . . . Sometimes I
am afraid to speak to him, lest I should be too frank, lest I should
seem forward: for I have more than once regretted bitterly, over-
flowing, superfluous words, and feared I had said more than he
expected me to say, and that he would disapprove what he might
deem my indiscretion" (S, I, 107–8). She is quite aware that her love
for Robert is hopeless: "Different, indeed, . . . is Robert's mental
condition to mine: I think only of him; he has no room, no leisure to
think of me. The feeling called love is and has been for two years the
predominant emotion of my heart; always there, always awake, always astir: quite other feelings absorb his reflections, and govern his
faculties" (S, I, 191).

Yet Caroline's knowledge of Robert's indifference does not free
her from emotional bondage; rather it condemns her not only to
suffering the agonies of unrequited love but also to despising herself
for transgressing the limits set by the society of which she is irrevocably a part: "She had loved without being asked to love,—a natural,
sometimes an inevitable chance, but big with misery" (S, I, 116).

Knowing that her society denies women the right to natural response and aware that the exchange of locks of hair with Robert was
at her instigation, she considers the act "one of those silly deeds it
distresses the heart and sets the face on fire to think of: one of those
small but sharp recollections that return, lacerating your self-
respect like tiny penknives, and forcing from your lips, as you sit
alone, sudden, insane-sounding interjections" (*S*, I, 251).

Her will and her courage are great: because "it was despicable,
she felt, to pine sentimentally, to cherish secret griefs, vain
memories" (*S*, I, 204), she forces herself to learn the brutal lesson of
stoicism:

Take the matter as you find it: ask no questions; utter no remonstrances; it is
your best wisdom. You expected bread, and you have got a stone; break
your teeth on it, and don't shriek because the nerves are martyrized: do not
doubt that your mental stomach . . . is as strong as an ostrich's—the stone
will digest. You held out your hand for an egg, and fate put into it a
scorpion. Show no consternation: close your fingers firmly upon the gift; let
it sting through your palm. Never mind: in time, after your hand and arm
have swelled and quivered long with torture, the squeezed scorpion will
die, and you will have learned the great lesson how to endure without a sob.
For the whole remnant of your life, if you survive the test—some, it is said,
die under it—you will be stronger, wiser, less sensitive. (*S*, *I*, 114)

But for Caroline, as for Jane Eyre, a life without love is meaningless and empty: "I wish somebody in the world loved me. . . . it is
scarcely *living* to measure time as I do. . . . The hours pass, and I
get them over somehow, but I do not *live*. I endure existence, but I
rarely enjoy it" (*S*, II, 63). She loses her desire to survive under such
conditions, and defining herself as "a poor, doomed mortal" who
"ought not to have been born, [or] should have [been] smothered
. . . at the first cry" (*S*, I, 256–57), she is hypnotized by the thought
of her impending physical dissolution: her mind "for ever runs on
the question, how she shall at last encounter, and by whom be
sustained through death?" (*S*, I, 256). It is "grief [not physical sickness that] is . . . [her] worst ailment," but having "no object in life"
(*S*, II, 121–22), she sinks into what threatens to be a fatal illness:

Life wastes fast in such vigils as Caroline had of late but too often kept; vigils
during which the mind,—having no pleasant food to nourish it . . . tries to
live on the meagre diet of wishes, and failing to derive thence either delight

or support, and feeling itself ready to perish with craving want, turns to philosophy, to resolution, to resignation; calls on all these gods for aid, calls vainly,—is unheard, unhelped, and languishes. (S, II, 36)

V   Shirley Keeldar's Story

Caroline's situation is, however, both less complicated and less tragic than that of Shirley Keeldar. Despising the role men ask her to play, Shirley attempts to stifle her sexual needs and refuses to marry because she knows that if she becomes a wife, "I could never be my own mistress more. A terrible thought!—it suffocates me!" (S, I, 235). Thus she tries, in so far as it is possible, to play a male role: she consistently speaks of herself as a man and adopts the sobriquet, "the first gentleman in Briarfield" (S, II, 16). Yet the context of the novel makes it plain that these acts are perverse and self-destructive; for intellectually, Shirley is an ardent feminist. She not only does not accept the inferior role deemed appropriate for women but adamantly asserts that women are by nature superior to their male rulers.

The traditional conceptualizations of Eve reveal what the male believes to be the essential qualities of the female. Innocent and unfallen Eve is conceived of as the mindless inferior of her male master, the lovely servant depicted by a Milton who, as Shirley bitterly asserts, "tried to see the first woman; but . . . saw her not. . . . It was his cook that he saw" (S, II, 2). But Eve, the quintessential woman, is seen in another aspect by men: she is also the fallen betrayer of humanity, the destroyer of her innocent mate. Rejecting both these stereotypes of Eve, Shirley twice presents her own impassioned descriptions of the first woman. She insists that far from being the inferior of the male, the woman is the source of life: "the first men of the earth were Titans, and . . . Eve was their mother: from her sprang Saturn, Hyperion, Oceanus; she bore Prometheus— . . . " (S, II, 2). And in her long essay on "the bridal-hour of Genius and Humanity" (S, II, 186), that is based on the description of the mating of the "sons of God" with "the daughters of men" in Genesis 6:1–4, Shirley denies the traditional antifeminist interpretation of the myth by linking it to the story of Cupid and Psyche and to the New Testament descriptions of the intervention of the triune Godhead in human affairs. Reversing the traditional male-female hierarchy, she attributes to women superior powers inhering in their sexuality, which she sees as the channel

through which the Divine spirit flows to ensoul flesh. The moment
of union is described in language which both echoes Scripture and is
infused with sexual meaning: accepting the spirit who seeks her out,
the woman responds first in the words of Mary at the Annunciation,
then in those of St. John in his prayer for Christ's return; and
ultimately she achieves apotheosis in an orgasmic experience shared
by all nature (*S*, II, 185–86).

Yet Shirley is unable to live in terms of this doctrine not because
society denies it—for blessed by wealth and beauty, she can live
independent of society's strictures—but because her own nature
betrays her. In one of the most painful of her many studies of the
conflict between mind and emotion, Charlotte depicts Shirley as
held prisoner in a psychological trap. For despite all of Shirley's
protestations that she is and must continue to be the equal of any
man, she admits that in choosing a mate, "I prefer a *master*. . . . A
man I shall feel it impossible not to love, and very possible to fear"
(*S*, II, 256).

For the greater part of the novel, Shirley, who is terrorized by her
desire to surrender herself to an aggressive male, adamantly insists
that she is not and never has been in love. Because she in truth feels
nothing but friendship for the masterful Robert Moore, she is able
not only to reject his proposal but also to assert her moral superiority over him on the grounds that in seeking to marry her not because
he loves her but because he wishes to share her wealth, he acts "like
a brigand," or a murderer who "would immolate me to that mill—
your Moloch" (*S*, II, 236–37). But she is unable to reject Robert's
brother, Louis, to whom she has long been passionately attracted.
The battle between Shirley and Louis, which is the center of interest in the last section of the novel, echoes the battle between
Jane and Rochester; and Louis' internal struggles are reminiscent of
those of William Crimsworth.

Knowing that marriage will entail psychological bondage, Shirley
uses the class difference between herself, an heiress, and Louis
Moore, the poor tutor of her nephew, as a defense against the
passionate desires she both yearns to fulfill and fears. She is insolent
to Louis because she believes *his* pride will keep him from propos-
ing and thereby risking a rebuff. And Louis does for a long while
remain silent; for although he believes she loves him, he feels that
"her Gold and her Station are two griffins, that guard her on each
side" (*S*, II, 327). For him as for Shirley, passion threatens the self;

and he vows that "if I must be her slave, I will not lose my freedom for nothing" (S, II, 228).

Ultimately, however, Louis chooses not to be a slave but to use the traits which are natural to a woman and which he defines as "faults and foibles," as the "steps by which I mount to ascendancy over her" (S, II, 223). He delights that he can look upon Shirley as "childish": "it was unutterably sweet to feel myself at once near her and above her: to be conscious of natural right and power to sustain her, as a husband should sustain a wife" (S, II, 223). Even as he struggles to subdue her, he exults in his self-mastery, reflecting, "I am blessed in that power to cover all inward ebullition with outward calm. . . . Pleasant is it to have the gift to proceed peacefully and powerfully in your course without alarming by one eccentric movement" (S, II, 323).

He is not cruel; indeed, he is honorable: "It was not my present intention to utter one word of love to her, or to reveal one glimpse of the fire in which I wasted. Presumptuous, I never have been; presumptuous, I never will be: rather than even *seem* selfish and interested, I would resolutely . . . part and leave her" (S, II, 324). For him, too, love demands a giving up, a surrender of pride: "You look hot and haughty," he accuses Shirley. She replies, "And you far haughtier. Yours is the monstrous pride which counterfeits humility" (S, II, 330). And here is the core of his problem: if he is to triumph, he must discard the protective mask of false humility donned to enable him to view rejection in sociological rather than personal terms; he must hazard himself in his proposal to her.

But in accepting his proposal, Shirley must surrender more than he. His very language clarifies the situation: anticipating her acceptance of him, he says, "I have tamed [the] lioness and am her keeper" (S, II, 323); and at the moment of her submission, he sees "she had felt insurrection, and was waking to empire" (S, II, 326). Louis' diary account of the brutal proposal scene in which he forces Shirley to give up pride, social conventions, and ultimately herself conveys Charlotte's belief that the woman's nature demands not merely that she surrender but that she be mastered:

"'You name me leopardess; remember, the leopardess is tameless,' said she.

"'Tame or fierce, wild or subdued, you are *mine*.'

" 'I am glad to know my keeper, and am used to him. Only his voice will I follow; only his hand shall manage me; only at his feet will I repose.' " (*S*, II, 337)

Shirley is driven to accept the loss of selfhood entailed in marriage by her sexual desire, which ultimately triumphs over her desire for independence; and Louis himself perceives the agony that her conflicting drives cause her: "Pantheress!—beautiful forest-born!—wily, tameless, peerless nature! She gnaws her chain: I see the white teeth working at the steel! She has dreams of her wild woods, and pinings after virgin freedom" (*S*, II, 343). Yet ultimately Shirley is, Charlotte asserts, "fettered to a fixed day: there she lay, conquered by love, and bound with a vow. Thus vanquished and restricted, she pined, like any other chained denizen of deserts. Her captor alone could cheer her; his society only could make amends for the lost privilege of liberty; in his absence, she sat or wandered alone; spoke little and ate less" (*S*, II, 352).

VI *The Prevailing Tone*

The final chapters of *Shirley* offer what are at best only partial solutions to the issues the novel has raised. Caroline, who had predicted that "if an abundant gush of happiness came on me, I could revive" (*S*, II, 122), is rescued from death by the love she feels for and receives from her long-lost mother. Robert—seriously wounded by the "half-crazed weaver" (*S*, II, 349), Michael Hartley—is forced to revaluate his past deeds and aims; and he concludes that although "formerly, pecuniary ruin was equivalent in my eyes to personal dishonour, it is not so now" (*S*, II, 306). Therefore, he proposes to Caroline, who gladly accepts him, happy to forfeit her dreams of independence and a career for what is to her the greater joy of love.

The last pages of the novel describe the English victory of 1812 and the repealing of the "Orders in Council." The acuteness of the economic crisis passed, Robert—who has seen "the necessity of doing good" (*S*, II, 358) with any wealth he may possess—will not be forced to decide between his own economic survival and the welfare of his employees. But this happy ending does not mitigate the bleakness of the vision that informs the novel. Charlotte has provided no answers to the complex problems with which she deals, for she believes there are no answers to give. The mills will continue to

be mechanized, as Robert himself predicts, and the mill workers
will go unemployed; the desperate situation of women, which is the
product of deep and enduring fear and which is justified by the
weight of the entire social and religious tradition of Western civiliza-
tion, will remain unaltered.

The novel's depiction of frustration, terror, and hatred is too powerful to be outweighed by the brief, almost laconic, conclusion
which describes the public victory celebration and the marriages of
the protagonists. No solution is offered to the plight of the millions
of unmated women who are "envious, backbiting, wretched, because life is a desert to them" (S, II, 84). Caroline's final happiness
in being chosen by Robert to be his wife is given far less emphasis
than were her bitter sufferings while he heartlessly ignored her; and
Shirley, who consents at last to become Mrs. Louis Moore, is to the
end presented as a defeated rebel who "gnaws" the "chain" (S, II,
343) of her own desires, which bind her. Charlotte has fulfilled her
desire to speak out on the " 'condition of women' question," and
that condition, as she sees it, is black indeed.

Shirley consistently has been considered the least successful of
the novels Charlotte Brontë published during her lifetime. Most
modern critics have agreed with contemporary reviewer George
Henry Lewes who stated that "in *Shirley* all unity . . . is wanting. . . . The various scenes are gathered up into three volumes,—
they have not grown into a work."[6] The shifting of interest in the
middle of the book from Caroline to Shirley and the fact that both
women are inevitably little more than bystanders in the sustaining
plot-conflict between employee and employer rob *Shirley* of dramatic force. *Jane Eyre* and *Villette* enclose the reader in the claustro-
phobic worlds created by the narrators' imagination which trans-
mutes melodramatic incident into symbol and subsumes mundane
event in internal joy and agony. The third-person point of view
through which the entwined stories of Caroline and Shirley are told,
inevitably sacrifices this self-involved intensity which can transform
an English country house and a Continental girls' school into
psychological chambers of horror.

Yet *Shirley* by no means lacks power and significance. By combin-
ing two romantic plots against a background of civil strife, Charlotte
transforms social theory into art. In *Jane Eyre*, Jane comments
briefly on the "millions [of women who] are condemned to a stiller
doom than mine and . . . are in silent revolt against that lot" (*JE*, I,

139). The stories of Caroline and Shirley, and those of the spinsters, daughters, wives, and mothers who surround them, powerfully dramatize this condition; moreover, the extended discussions of their days of busy idleness which leads to mental and physical illness effectively lay bare the flawed nature of their society.

No less than the women, the militant mill workers and mill owners are victims of a social code which praises the virtues of aggressive independence and action, but which deprives the individual of opportunities to develop and to exercise these capacities. *Shirley* is a chronicle of frustrated energies—Caroline Helstone's near death from enforced passivity epitomizes the threat which hangs over all. Chained by tradition, men can assert their maleness only by becoming ruthless rulers—Robert of his workers, Louis of the woman he loves. Taught to admire this capacity to exercise power, women must inculcate, cherish, and approve those very qualities in their men which prevent both sexes from achieving their full human potential. The passages which describe Caroline's slow decline into neurasthenic illness and Shirley's agonized equivocation over Louis Moore's proposal not only probe deeply into the divisive ambivalence of the psyche, but also expose the life-denying, death-seeking quality of the social ethos. Robert Moore's insistence that he must forego both passion and charity in the interest of economic survival and Louis' awareness that he must bind Shirley with psychological chains if he is to wed her, expose the link between the ego, economic power, and sexual power. Though *Shirley* provides no solutions to the problems it illuminates, it effectively expresses a felt knowledge of despair and frustration.

CHAPTER 6

Villette

I *The Plot*

Villette, in which Charlotte returned to her Brussels experience, is the story of a woman's struggle for survival against virtually insuperable odds. The novel opens with fourteen-year-old Lucy Snowe's extended visit to her godmother, Louisa Bretton, and her sixteen-year-old son, Graham. When an old friend, Mr. Home, brings his daughter Polly to stay with Mrs. Bretton while he is away on a long journey, she pays far more attention to her new guest than to Lucy, who retreats to the sidelines. Polly, heartbroken by her father's departure and desperately lonely, transfers her affections to Graham, who treats her with careless kindness. Lucy, asserting stoical indifference, closely observes these relationships in which she has no active part.

Lucy's story recommences after a passage of eight years, during which time her family has perished in some never-explained disaster, and she has lost touch with Mrs. Bretton, who has suffered financial reverses. Forced to be independent but without any training with which to earn a living, Lucy becomes a companion to an embittered invalid, Miss Marchmont. Gradually, a friendship develops between the two women, and Miss Marchmont decides to provide for Lucy's future; however, before she can put this plan into effect, she dies; and Lucy is again left to fend for herself.

Aware that England offers her no opportunities and having heard that foreign girls are prized as children's nurses by her compatriots, she decides to use her small savings to journey to the Continent where she hopes to find a similar position. On the channel boat she meets a young girl named Ginevra Fanshawe, who attends a school in Villette and who suggests that Lucy might apply for work as nurse to the children of the school's owner, Madame Beck. After a single night in the port city in which she disembarked, Lucy, having no better plan in mind, decides to seek out Madame Beck; but Ginevra, when she casually suggested Lucy do so, failed to give her any directions for finding the school. On the journey to Villette, Lucy's luggage is misplaced; and she finds herself alone, virtually penniless, and without any clear idea of where she wishes to go in the city. Puzzled and frightened, she stumbles through the dark streets until she arrives at a lighted door which she finds to her surprise is the entrance to Madame Beck's *Pensionnat de Demoiselles*. Feeling she has been guided by Providence, Lucy knocks and asks for employment; and Madame Beck, after a brief consultation with her cousin, Paul Emanuel, hires Lucy to be her children's nurse.

Lucy settles into a quiet routine: she observes the life of the school and pays particular attention to a young physician, Dr. John, who is frequently in attendance upon one of Mrs. Beck's children. Lucy also remains friendly with Ginevra, who makes of her a confidant and tells her that she is being courted by a man she refers to as Isidore, but that she cares nothing for him. Madame Beck carefully watches Lucy; and having discovered that her new employee possesses intelligence and strength of character, she urges her to become the English teacher of the school. Thus Lucy finds herself beginning a new career.

One night while she is walking alone in the garden of the school, Lucy is surprised when a casket is dropped at her feet from the window of the boys' school adjacent to the *pensionnat* grounds. In the box there is a love letter, and Lucy realizes that she has been mistaken for some pupil. While she is pondering what to do, Dr. John arrives; and insisting that the girl for whom the letter is meant is innocent of any wrongdoing, he begs Lucy not to speak of the incident. Lucy agrees, but wonders whether Dr. John is the writer and whom among the students he wishes to protect. When she eventually discovers that he is Ginevra's mysterious suitor, Isidore, she can understand neither why he loves so silly a girl nor why Ginevra scorns his attentions.

When the long vacation begins, Lucy is left alone in the school. The depression caused by her lonely condition increases, and at last she suffers so acutely that one evening in desperation she runs from the building which hallucinations have made horrible to her and walks through the city. Impulsively, she enters a Roman Catholic church, and spontaneously goes to the confessional, where she pours out her despair. Leaving the church, she is overcome by weakness and faints.

She recovers consciousness in a room which seems hauntingly familiar; and soon she discovers that she has been found unconscious by Dr. John, who has brought her to the house he shares with his mother. The suspicions Lucy has entertained for some time are now confirmed: Dr. John is indeed Graham Bretton. Asked by both mother and son why she did not identify herself on one of his many visits to the school, Lucy explains that his obvious failure to recognize her had kept her from claiming acquaintance. However, she delights in her new-found friends and spends a number of happy weeks with them. During the period, she several times meets M. Emanuel, who goes out of his way to criticize both her and Dr. John; and Lucy, cherishing her new happiness, resents his officious intrusion into her life.

Against her will, Lucy falls in love with Dr. John; and when she returns to labor at Madame Beck's school, she breathlessly awaits the letters he has promised her. When at last a letter arrives, Lucy, desiring to read and savor it in private, takes it to the attic of the school; but before she can do more than glance at it, she is terrified to see before her the figure of a nun. The school is rumored to be haunted by such a ghost; and convinced that she has seen a supernatural being, Lucy runs from the room, leaving behind her precious letter. She pours out her story to Madame Beck and her visitors, of whom Dr. John is one; and he suggests that she may be suffering from hallucinations.

Frightened for her sanity and despairingly aware that Dr. John feels nothing more than friendship for her, Lucy struggles with little success to extirpate her love for him. One evening she accompanies him to the theater. A fire breaks out, and he helps to rescue a young woman who is in danger of being crushed by the stampeding crowd. Soon it is discovered that this lady, the Countess Paulina Mary, and her father, the Count de Bassompierre, are Mr. Home and his daughter, Polly. Having succeeded to a French title, he has for years made his home in Europe and has lost touch with his English acquaintances, whom he is pleased to meet again.

Although Lucy is frequently asked to attend social gatherings with the two families, her loneliness and sadness increase as she becomes aware that Dr. John is losing all interest in her and is falling more and more in love with Paulina, who returns his affection. Lucy forces herself to accept the fact that Dr. John will soon marry another: in a symbolic act, she sadly buries the letters that he has written to her; and as she does so, the figure of the nun reappears, filling her with terror. Meanwhile, Paul Emanuel, who teaches some classes at his cousin's school, has been showing interest in Lucy. Short-tempered and hard to please, he consistently criticizes her, but he also treats her kindly. Lucy is both angered and amused by his peremptory authoritarianism, but she truly respects his mind. Gradually, the two are drawn together; and at last Paul pledges his firm friendship and asks her to consider him as an adopted brother.

Shortly thereafter, Madame Beck asks Lucy to take some fruit to an aged acquaintance, Madame Walravens. The old woman is, as Lucy soon discovers, the grandmother of the girl Paul once wished to marry. Her family had rejected his suit, and the girl, Justine Marie, had entered a convent and had died soon thereafter. Her family then suffered financial reverses; and Paul, far from harboring vengeance, cared for them and for many years has maintained a home with his confessor, Père Silas, for the old woman who was once his bitterest enemy. Once she is told this story by Père Silas, Lucy realizes that her growing love for Paul will be opposed both by his family and his church; and indeed, Paul does become more distant to her. She hears that he will soon leave on an extended journey to the West Indies to care for his family's financial interests, and she wonders if he has succumbed so totally to his friends' and relatives' desires that he will leave her without a word. As she waits in sickening suspense, her life takes on a nightmare quality.

Determined that her cousin Paul shall remain unmarried and aware that Lucy is being made desperate by the fact he is soon to leave, Madame Beck drugs her in an effort to keep her passive. But stimulated rather than sedated by the draught she is given, Lucy wanders at night to the city park which is lighted for a festival. There she sees Paul surrounded by Père Silas, Madame Walravens, and Madame Beck. From overheard snatches of conversation, Lucy discovers that they are awaiting the arrival of Justine Marie; and in her overwrought state, Lucy assumes that they expect the specter bride to claim her bridegroom. Lucy prepares to confront this horror; but when a young and clearly mortal girl appears, Lucy realizes that it is Paul's goddaughter, Justine Marie, for whom they have been waiting. The sight of Paul increases both Lucy's love and despair, and she returns to the school where she finds what seems to be the body of a nun lying on her bed. Driven to desperation by the emotional crisis she is undergoing, this time Lucy does not run from the apparition; instead she advances toward it and finds the mysterious shape is only a bolster dressed in a nun's garb. The following morning, it is discovered that Ginevra has eloped with a young nobleman, and she reveals in a note to Lucy that her lover frequently had visited her in the school disguised as a nun.

Lucy's fear that she is subject to hallucinations born of madness is now allayed, but she continues to suffer, for the time of Paul's departure is drawing near, and he has made no sign to her. On the afternoon of his last day at the school, goaded past endurance, Lucy thrusts herself between Madame Beck and Paul and announces her heartbroken grief. Paul turns to her, invites her to accompany him on a walk, takes her to a small house fitted up as school, and announces that he has arranged for her to run it in his absence. When he declares his love for her and asks her to marry him, Lucy joyfully accepts his proposal, pledges to execute faithfully all his wishes while he is gone and to await cheerfully his return. But the novel ends with the description of a great storm which arises while Paul is on his return voyage and which strews the ocean with wrecks. Lucy is alone once more.

II   The Controlling Vision

Villette, the spiritual autobiography of a deeply neurotic woman, is the blackest of Charlotte Brontë's novels. The third-person omniscient point of view of *Shirley* serves to objectify the tragic vision which informs that work, but *Villette* is a detailed record of finely differentiated degrees of emotional pain experienced by the protagonist, Lucy Snowe, as she tells her own story. Her suffering, therefore, seems both immediate and absolute, for the world of the novel is limited to the grasp of this single, agonized consciousness. Lucy's concern is not so much with what happens as with how she feels about what happens, and the series of misfortunes she suffers fills her with such pain and fear that she consistently perceives her world through a distorting veil of terror. Life is to her a "war,"[1] a "desert" (V, I, 71); she considers herself a castaway, a pilgrim, a doomed victim of hidden, threatening forces.[2]

As a result, the novel is suffused with an atmosphere of confusion and despair. Because she hates and fears the alien Continental culture of Villette, Lucy defines it as sick and evil. To her, the "strange, frolicsome noisy little world" of the Roman Catholic school where she teaches epitomizes the corrupt system of which it is a sustaining part: "great pains were taken to hide chains with flowers. . . . the CHURCH strove to bring up her children robust in body, feeble in soul, fat, ruddy, hale, joyous, ignorant, unthinking, unquestioning. . . . 'Look after your bodies; leave your souls to me. I hold their cure—guide their course: I guarantee their final fate.' . . . Lucifer just offers the same terms" (V, I, 158). She considers the clean, comfortable school building to be an imprisoning "dungeon" (V, II, 258), a "strange house [where it is not] possible to find security or secresy" (V, II, 56); and the garden which surrounds the *pensionnat* seems to be a threatening maze where "the eyes of the flowers had gained vision, and the knots in the tree boles listened like secret ears" (V, I, 143).

From the beginning, Lucy believes the sagacious, successful Madame Beck to be a figure of menace—a "Minos in petticoats" (V, I, 86), who "in her own single person . . . could have comprised the duties of a first minister and a superintendent of police" (V, I, 89). As a result, Lucy interprets her employer's legitimate attempts to be cognizant of all that occurs in her school as revelatory of a malevolent nature: to Lucy's eyes, Madame Beck is a "huntress," "stealing like a cat round the garden" (V, I, 141). And although Lucy is involved only to the extent of having been an innocent and unwilling witness to Dr. John Bretton's surreptitious entry into the school grounds, she feels that merely by being present, she has become the helpless victim of her employer: "a delicious little ravelled plot lay tempting [Madame Beck] to disentanglement; and in the midst, folded round and round in cobwebs, had she not secured 'Meess Lucie,' clumsily involved, like the foolish fly she was?" (V, I, 142).

The fear which constantly haunts Lucy, while it sometimes leads her to what are clearly hallucinatory visions, is not, however, without some basis in fact. Her sufferings are real enough and are, in great measure, the result of accident or unalterable circumstance. She is orphaned, and she lacks both money and powerful friends. Therefore, although she is not "of a self-reliant or active nature" (V, I, 40), her circumstances force her to exert herself and make her aware that until she can provide for herself, she will feel with every day that passes "the peril (of destitution) nearer, the conflict (for existence) more severe" (V, I, 68). Her lack of beauty and rank, given Dr. John's predilections, makes it impossible for him to respond to her aching love for him. The combined urgings of his family and his conscience separate Paul Emanuel from her, and the tempest that overwhelms his returning vessel makes their separation absolute.

Thus, even if Lucy's recollections of her past were presented in the most objective terms, they would form a record of defeat and loss. Unlike Charlotte's other protagonists, who share both her unfortunate circumstances and her passionate need for physical love, Lucy is forever thwarted. Her somber analysis of her emotional state when Miss Marchmont dies is an accurate prophecy of what she will experience again and again: "It seemed I must be stimulated into action. I must be goaded, driven, stung, forced to energy. My little morsel of human affection, which I prized as if it were a solid pearl, must melt in my fingers and slip thence like a dissolving hailstone" (V, I, 43).

The darker quality of this, the last of Charlotte's novels, is perhaps most easily recognized through comparison with *Jane Eyre*. Again and again, Jane moves from a place outside of or on the very fringe of the social circle to a position of control in the center. As a child, she is isolated as an inferior from her cousins and the grand company that visits them; but she returns in triumph to Gateshead Hall to witness the death of her tyrant aunt and the disintegration of the family that had cruelly robbed her of her social position and her inheritance. At Lowood, she ascends from ignominy to the position of "first girl of the first class"; at Thornfield, she exchanges her status of lowly governess for that of fiancée of the master; and when her story ends, she reigns supreme, even over Rochester, as the mistress of their private world which contains within its bounds all that satisfies her "sweetest wishes." Tempted to remain passive under adversity, when at last she is stung into action, Jane finds that "energy" commands "obedience": her will is sufficient to subdue the inimical forces around her.

Lucy, unlike Jane, achieves no such triumphs: unspecified disaster deprives her of her real family; her surrogate mother, Miss Marchmont, is taken from her by death; Dr. John turns from her to another woman; and Paul is drowned. Far more inclined to passivity than Jane, Lucy finds that when she is forced to act and to feel, she only suffers more acutely than when she does nothing. Unable to stifle what she has always known is a hopeless love for Dr. John, she discovers that although "solitude is sadness," "life . . . has worse than that. Deeper than melancholy, lies heartbreak" (*V*, II, 224).

The essential difference in these two novels lies in Charlotte's own changing perception of the nature of human experince. *Jane Eyre* is a version of the Cinderella fairy tale: Jane achieves wealth and position through no act of her own, and she plays no part in the event which removes the impediment to her marriage. Moreover, Jane feels free to impose her will on others and to place happiness in this life above the fate of her immortal soul; and within the context of the novel, dominated as it is by her consciousness, this decision, which leads to happiness, is applauded.

But *Villette*, written five years later, is suffused with the somber religious philosophy which Charlotte, in her depression and grief, had embraced as her own. Lucy acknowledges that she is one of many "travellers" who "encounter weather fitful and gusty, wild and variable—breast adverse winds, are belated and overtaken by the early closing winter night," yet she asserts, "neither can this happen without the sanction of God" (*V*, II, 160). Charlotte herself clung desperately to this hard, religious creed which neither denies nor alleviates the day-to-day agonies of the believer, but demands that he endure them in the faith that they are a necessary part of the Creator's perfect and immutable plan. Charlotte's letters are filled with comments similar to those she addressed to Mr. William S. Williams shortly after Anne's death, when she remarked, "why life is so black, brief, and bitter I do not know. . . . but I believe God is wise—perfect—merciful."[3]

Charlotte's treatment of Lucy is complex, perceptive, and unsentimental: on the one hand, she consistently insists that Lucy is to a great degree the victim of accidental misfortunes and unjustified cruelties practiced upon her by an unfeeling and perverse society; on the other hand, Charlotte recognizes and even insists that Lucy's neuroticism is a cause of much of her suffering and that she is, therefore, in part responsible for the constant agony she feels. It is, of course, easy to place too much weight on Lucy's habitually neurotic cast of mind and consequently to assume that her determined struggle to achieve Christian resignation is either the cause or the effect of her precarious mental balance, but such a reading is not supported by the author or by the novel.

Charlotte's remark to her publisher that Lucy "*is* both morbid and weak at times"; that "her character sets up no pretensions to un-mixed strength," and that "anybody living her life would necessarily become morbid,"[4] indicates that she was fully conscious of Lucy's mental instability; indeed, *Villette* is filled with statements in which Lucy acknowledges an awareness of her defective condition. She comments again and again about her perversity (*V*, I, 121; II, 112, 170); she sadly admits that "mine [is] a soon-depressed, an easily-deranged temperament" (*V*, II, 82); and in despair she echoes the Psalmist saying, "From my youth up Thy terrors have I suffered with a troubled mind" (*V*, I, 201).

But Charlotte insists that Lucy's incapacitating psychological problems are neither the sole cause of her troubles nor an excuse which can absolve her of responsibility for either her beliefs or her actions. Rather, this facet of her heroine's nature is viewed by Char-lotte merely as one fact which, considered with her other qualities, influences her ability to deal with the situation in which she is placed. Her lack of money forces her into labor for which she is unsuited; her lack of beauty deprives her of the power to win the love of the man of whom she is enamored; her "troubled mind" robs her of the ability to handle effectively the exigencies of daily existence in her brutal society and, far more important, drives her to the verge of a spiritual despair which condemns its sufferer to a life of negative withdrawal that "blaspheme[s] the Creator" (*V*, I, 48).

Villette is, therefore, more than a sensitive study of the vagaries of a disturbed mind: the narrative is Charlotte's brilliant attempt to confront eternal spiritual questions. Lucy's problem is that of Job—how is man to respond to what seems to be unjustified, in-explicable, and endless suffering—and Charlotte skillfully con-structs her novel to illuminate the answer that she had herself found and to which she steadfastly adhered. A statement by Miss March-mont provides the philosophical framework for the entire novel: a life of pain teaches the essential truth that "we should acknowledge God merciful, but not always for us comprehensible. We should accept our own lot whatever it be, and try to render happy that of others" (*V*, I, 48). This rule is the one by which Paul Emanuel also lives, and his faithfulness to this creed makes Lucy love and revere him as her "Christian hero" (*V*, II, 188).

As the language of the novel makes clear, Lucy's story, on one level, records her spiritual growth. Although she "had wanted to compromise with Fate—to escape occasional great agonies by submitting to a whole life of privation and small pains"—she finds that "fate would not be so pacified; nor would providence sanction this shrinking sloth and cowardly indolence" (*V*, I, 43). For Lucy, as "for most" "Pilgrims," the path of life stretches "dark through the wilderness of this world" (*V*, II, 240); and her lonely journey to Europe, where she will be forced to confront directly the terrors she has wished to shun, is described, appropriately enough, as a voyage of the soul to the underworld: "Down the sable flood we glided; I thought of the Styx, and of Charon rowing some solitary soul to the Land of Shades" (*V*, I, 58–59).

III   *The Awakening Consciousness*

The opening chapters of *Villette*, which establish Lucy's character and reveal her social and economic status, epitomize Charlotte's treatment of her heroine. Recognizing that Lucy's difficulties are the product of a myriad of inextricably related causes, Charlotte makes it immediately clear that there is no solution to Lucy's dilemma, for she is caught in a vicious circle: robbed of hope and made fearful by circumstances over which she has no control, she exacerbates her situation by retreating into a negative passivity which increases her vulnerability both to inimical external forces and to her own latent self-destructive impulses. This attitude is depicted in the first three chapters which detail the events of a few months of Lucy's fourteenth year when, hovering between childhood and adulthood, she begins to define herself and the nature of experience. Given the specificity of her memories, the fact that Lucy never mentions either her father or her mother, remarking only that she had been living with "kinsfolk" (*V*, I, 2), implies that she has long been deprived of parental love.

Her despairing belief that she will never be the object of deep affection is suggested by her insistence that she is deeply satisfied with the unemotional kindness of her godmother, Mrs. Bretton: "I liked the visit. The house and the inmates specially suited me. . . . One child in a household of grown people is usually made very much of, and in a quiet way I was a good deal taken notice of by Mrs.

Bretton" (V, I, 1). But Lucy is not for long the center of even this temperate interest; the "peace" that she "liked . . . so well" (V, I, 2) is disturbed almost at once by the arrival first of little Polly Home and then of Graham, Mrs. Bretton's son; and Lucy soon finds herself become an onlooker who is forced to witness highly emotional scenes in which she plays no part. Polly's grief at being separated from her adored father makes her the object of more loving attention than Lucy has ever received: "Mrs. Bretton was not generally a caressing woman: even with her deeply-cherished son, her manner was rarely sentimental, often the reverse; but when the small stranger smiled at her, she kissed it" (V, I, 5).

As the days pass, Lucy devotes herself to analyzing the child who has usurped her place. Carefully masking her jealous animosity by adopting an attitude of cold superiority and objectivity, she insists that "these sudden, dangerous natures . . . offer many a curious spectacle to those whom a cooler temperament has secured from participation in their angular vagaries." Thus when Mr. Home unexpectedly returns for a visit, and Polly, spying him from the window, "like a bird or a shaft, or any other swift thing, . . . [flies] from the room," Lucy watches "calmly"; and although she believes "that the child [has] run out mad, and ought instantly to be pursued" (V, I, II), she limits her response to toying with the idea of announcing these conclusions to Mrs. Bretton. Having no parents of her own, Lucy observes the family drama which unfolds about her with both puzzlement and envy. Observing how Mr. Home silently "nestled" his child on his knee for "an hour," she remarks, "I suppose both were satisfied" (V, I, 13); and as she watches Polly assiduously caring for her father's slightest needs, she summarizes her own bitter frustration by saying, "Candidly speaking, I thought her a little busy-body; but her father, blind like other parents, seemed perfectly content to let her wait on him, and even wonderfully soothed by her offices. 'She is my comfort!' he could not help saying to Mrs. Bretton. That lady had her own 'comfort' and nonpareil on a much larger scale . . . ; so she sympathized with his foible" (V, I, 14).

When Mr. Home leaves on an extended journey, the parting between father and daughter leads Mrs. Bretton to "shed a tear or two"; but Lucy insists, "I . . . was calm [although] I perceived [Polly] endured agony" (V, I, 22). Indeed, there is the clear suggestion throughout this opening section of the novel that by witnessing the suffering which the deeply affectionate Polly undergoes, Lucy is confirmed in her belief that one must repress emotions if one is to avoid pain. When, having turned to Graham in her father's absence, Polly "gathered [him] in her little arms," Lucy remembers that "the action . . . struck me as strangely rash; exciting the feeling one might experience on seeing an animal dangerous by nature, and but half-tamed by art, too heedlessly fondled. . . . I thought she ran a risk of incurring such a careless, impatient repulse, as would be worse to her than a blow" (V, I, 31).

Lucy is determined to risk no such danger for herself. Graham Bretton, handsome and two years her senior, makes it clear that she "fails[s] to yield" him "that precious commodity called amusement" (V, I, 16); and Lucy is careful never to acknowledge that his rejection means anything to her. Indeed, when Polly asks her if she "like[s] him much?" she acidly remarks, "I told you I liked him a little. Where is the use of caring for him so very much: he is full of faults. . . . Wise people say it is folly to think anybody perfect; and as to likes and dislikes, we should be friendly to all, and worship none" (V, I, 37). Yet the comment she makes some ten years later reveals that this studied indifference is a carefully assumed, defensive mask; staring at the portrait of Graham as he was when she visited in his home, she admits that his was "a most pleasant face to look at. . . . Any romantic little school-girl might have loved it in its frame" (VI, I, 213–14).

Afraid to risk herself, Lucy uses Polly to test the rightness of the philosophy of life which she has adopted. Observing that the child is "tractable" and quiet, "never kindling once to originality, or showing a single gleam of the peculiarities of her nature" when she is separated from the objects of her love, Lucy "ceased to watch her under such circumstances: she was not interesting" (V, I, 24). But she quietly intervenes again and again to make her a more "interesting" subject. Having concluded that Graham is a "spoiled, whimsical boy" (V, I, 15) and having observed that Polly—who seemed to have "no mind or life of her own, but must necessarily live, move, and have her being in another," Lucy urges her to interrupt the boy while he is engaged with his friends and so subjects Polly to a careless rebuff which breaks her heart. And when the message comes that Polly is to leave the Brettons to rejoin her father, Lucy "wonder[s]" (V, I, 31) how Polly will respond: she takes it upon herself to communicate the news; and she poses a series of questions

in order "to ascertain more of what she thought" (V, I, 34). The
conclusion she reaches on witnessing Polly's misery at being forced
to leave Graham confirm her fearful conviction that life is a "battle"
in which "shocks and repulses, . . . humiliations and desolation . . . are prepared for all flesh" (V, I, 38).

Subsequent events in Lucy's life support these conclusions of her
youth. When an unspecified disaster deprives her of family, she
defines herself as a drowning, shipwrecked sailor cast adrift on the
sea of tragic experience:

On quitting Bretton . . . I betook myself home. . . . Picture me then
idle, basking, plump, and happy, stretched on a cushioned deck, warmed
with constant sunshine, rocked by breezes indolently soft. However, . . . I
must somehow have fallen over-board, or . . . there must have been a
wreck at last. I too well remember a time—a long time—of cold, of danger,
of contention. To this hour, when I have the nightmare, it repeats the rush
and saltness of briny waves in my throat, and their icy pressure on my
lungs. I even know there was a storm, and that not of one hour nor one day.
For many days and nights neither sun nor stars appeared; we cast with our
own hands the tackling out of the ship; a heavy tempest lay on us; all hope
that we should be saved was taken away. In fine, the ship was lost, the crew
perished. (V, I, 39)

IV   *Repression and the Divided Self*

Her childhood apprehensions thus given specific form and her
terror justified by experience, Lucy enters upon adult life determined to repress half her nature. Despite the fact that she feels "life
at life's sources" (V, I, 41), she attempts to stifle the longings that
she feels will probably never be satisfied. Although her heart sinks
with her realization that in becoming Miss Marchmont's nurse-
companion, she will be condemned "to live here, in this close room,
the watcher of suffering, sometimes, perhaps, the butt of temper,
through all that was to come of my youth" (V, I, 41), she accepts her
lot with resignation: "Two hot, close rooms thus became my world;
and a crippled old woman my mistress, my friend, my all. . . . I
forgot that there were fields, woods, rivers, seas, an ever-changing
sky outside the steam-dimmed lattice of [the] sick-chamber; I was
almost content to forget it" (V, I, 42).

As a result, her recitation of her experiences becomes a record of
deep internal strife. When Miss Marchmont's death deprives Lucy
of this sterile safety and drives her to seek in a foreign land the

means of making a living, her long-subdued nature eagerly responds to the challenge: "In spite of my solitude, my poverty, and my perplexity, my heart, nourished and nerved with the vigour of a youth that had not yet counted twenty-three summers, beat light and not feebly" (V, I, 50). For a time, the very fact that she has no choice *but* to act overpowers the forces that have inhibited her—as she remarks, "mine was the game where the player cannot lose and may win" (V, I, 71). Thus she fluctuates between excitement and fear. Her position may rise before her "like a ghost," "anomalous, desolate, almost blank of hope" (V, I, 54); but her awareness that she is beginning a new chapter in her life invigorates her: "my inner self moved; my spirit shook its always-fettered wings half loose; I had a sudden feeling as if I who had never yet truly lived, were at last to taste life: in that morning my soul grew as fast as Jonah's gourd" (V, I, 55).

Yet, despite her excitement, Lucy is aware that "the cloud of doubt would be as thick to-morrow as ever" (V, I, 68); therefore, she chooses to respond in Villette as she had in England. Seeking no more than safety, she suppresses all desire for success and happiness: "with my usual base habit of cowardice, I shrunk into my sloth, like a snail into its shell, and alleged incapacity and impracticability as a pretext to escape action. . . . Not that true contentment dignified this infatuated resignation . . . ; but it seemed to me a great thing to be without heavy anxiety, and relieved from ultimate trial; the negation of severe suffering was the nearest approach to happiness I expected to know" (V, I, 92).

Indeed, Lucy takes a kind of pride in her ability to disguise from prying eyes what she conceives to be her true nature. In the past, she delighted in the fact that her "staid manner" had "enabled [her] to achieve with impunity, and even approbation, deeds that if attempted with an excited and unsettled air, would in some minds have stamped me as a dreamer and zealot" (V, I, 50). And, in Villette, she professes herself satisfied that her passivity should make her an enigma: knowing that she is accorded "just that degree of notice and consequence a person of my exterior habitually expects: that is to say, about what is given to unobtrusive articles of furniture," she feels free to observe intently the fascinating Dr. John who "never remembered that I had eyes in my head; much less a brain behind them" (V, I, 120).

But Lucy discovers to her horror that the priviate self which she has been eager to hide from the inquisitive and unfriendly eyes of the world is itself a mask behind which lurk powerful impulses, desires, and fears that are not subject to the control of her rational mind and that threaten to drive her into madness. Her sufferings have driven her to conclude that it is part of God's "great plan that some must deeply suffer while they live, and I thrilled in the certainty that of this number, I was one" (V, I, 198). But rather than accept this suffering which she believes is her God-ordained lot, she wills herself to feel nothing: "About the present, it was better to be stoical; about the future—such a future as mine—to be dead. And in catalepsy and a dead trance, I studiously held the quick of my nature" (V, I, 134). She is, however, unable to stifle totally her natural responses; against her will, she finds herself filled with a desire "for something to fetch me out of my present existence, and lead me upwards and onwards." She insists that "this longing, and all of a similar kind, it was necessary to knock on the head"; and she ruthlessly does so, "figuratively, after the manner of Jael to Sisera, driving a nail through their temples." Yet she must admit that "unlike Sisera, they did not die; they were but transiently stunned, and at intervals would turn on the nail with a rebellious wrench; then did the temples bleed, and the brain thrill to its core" (V, I, 135).

She professes herself well pleased to accept passively a life of privation because "I seemed to hold two lives—the life of thought, and that of reality; and, provided the former was nourished with a sufficiency of the strange necromantic joys of fancy, the privileges of the latter might remain limited to daily bread, hourly work, and a roof of shelter" (V, I, 92–93). But she finds that the fancy does not function merely to provide material for the "life of thought"— rather, since it is dominated by the subconscious, at times of great emotional stress, weakness, or exhaustion, it floods her mind with images of terror and despair. Even during moments of pleasure, she has a "ceaseless consciousness of anxiety lying in wait on enjoyment, like a tiger crouched in a jungle. The breathing of that beast of prey was in my ear always; his fierce heart panted close against mine; he never stirred in his lair but I felt him: I knew he waited only for sun-down to bound ravenous from his ambush" (V, I, 71). As her physical frame weakens, damaged by constant unhappiness and the conflict between will and passion, she is more and more victimized by mental terrors. Defining herself as "loverless and inexpectant of love" (V, I, 147), Lucy adamantly forces herself to remain "a mere looker-on at life" (*V*, I, 176); but when "the prop of employment [is] withdrawn" (*V*, I, 196) during the long school vacation, all her long suppressed desires and fears burst forth; and she suffers a physical and mental breakdown.

Determined to escape suffering by retreating from all experience that will arouse her feelings, Lucy becomes the unsuspecting and defenseless prey of her imagination which, liberated from the control of the rational faculty by her physical weakness, now alters her perception of reality. She has looked upon life metaphorically as "a hopeless desert" (*V*, I, 197); and to her terror, the physical world about her begins to conform to her trope: "The solitude and the stillness of the long dormitory could not be borne any longer; the ghastly white beds were turning into spectres—the coronal of each became a death's head, huge and sun-bleached—dead dreams of an elder world and mightier race lay frozen in their wide gaping eye-holes" (*V*, I, 201).

These visions of emptiness, sterility, and alienation from the love of God and man which now fill Lucy's mind drive her to the breaking point; and in a terror of guilt and fear, she seeks "any opening for appeal to God" (*V*, I, 202). Her agonized "confession" is a prelude to a total physical collapse which is brought on by a despair so complete that when she regains consciousness, her "soul" "re-entered her prison with pain, with reluctance. . . . The divorced mates, Spirit and Substance, were hard to re-unite: they greeted each other, not in an embrace, but a racking sort of struggle. . . . Consciousness revived in fear . . . " (*V*, I, 207).

V *Self-Torture and Cultural Victimization*

The second volume of *Villette* records Lucy's desperate struggle to control those emotions which she has learned that she can no longer totally suppress. Before, when her fear had focused on exterior forces, she had believed that she was pursued by evil or heartless people and watched by malign eyes; now, she feels threatened by her own nature. Her terrified response to the specter nun is based upon her fear that "she came out of my brain, and is now gone in there, and may glide out again at an hour and a day when I look not for her" (*V*, I, 316). It is appropriate, therefore, that this section of the novel opens with Lucy's prayer that if she must be subject to overwhelming emotional storms, she may at least be saved from sinking into guilty despair over her inability to repress those feelings which she now regards as part of the nature God himself has given her: "take [such feelings] to your Maker—show Him the secrets of the spirit He gave—ask Him how you are to bear the pains He has appointed—kneel in His presence, and pray with faith for light in darkness, for strength in piteous weakness, for patience in extreme need" (V, I, 225).

Charlotte shrewdly and sympathetically discerns that Lucy both suffers through no fault of her own and is herself responsible for her increasing trials. When queried by Dr. John as to the reason for her breakdown, Lucy pours out "a dreary, desperate complaint"; but she also insists that "it is no living being's fault." When he asks, "Who is in the wrong then, Lucy?" she responds, "Me . . . me; and a great abstraction on whose wide shoulders I like to lay the mountains of blame they were sculptured to bear: me and Fate" (V, I, 233). And Lucy is, of course, correct in her analysis: her acute frustration and despair are the result of the fact that without encouragement from Dr. John, she has fallen passionately in love with him. Recognizing that even to hope he will continue his compassionate kindness to her is to indulge in "insane . . . credulity" (V, I, 289), she forces herself to listen to the counseling voice of Reason, which, to her cry, "But if I feel, may I never express?" returns the answer, "Never!" (V, I, 290). Even her answers to his friendly letters must, she decides, be staid and brief: "Hope no delight of heart—no indulgence of intellect: grant no expansion to feeling—give holiday to no single faculty: dally with no friendly exchange: foster no genial intercommunion" (V, I, 289).

The ensuing description of Lucy's struggle to suppress the wish-fulfilling visions produced by her imagination is the most fully elaborated of Charlotte's many discussions of the tension between the rational and the imaginative faculties; and Lucy, like the protagonists of the other novels, shares Charlotte's ambivalent feelings toward these two opposed forces.[5] Imagination is Reason's "soft, bright foe, *our* sweet Help. . . . [a] divine, compassionate, succourable influence." Yet the delusive visions it creates, while they offer seemingly essential hope to the spirit fainting with "deadly weariness," "paralyzed [with] despair" (V, I, 290–91), are ultimately dangerous. When Lucy succumbs to the fierce impulse to dream and to hope, she falls into what she recognizes is "strange, sweet insanity" (V, I, 304).

Charlotte describes the power of Lucy's imagination in the terms she had once applied to the influence of her waking-dreams of Angria: insidiously delicious, the vision is like a narcotic drug, a "well-beloved poison" (*V*, I, 294), that addicts one by its very power to blot out painful reality—appeasing the soul's hunger "with food, sweet and strange" (*V*, I, 291) but sapping the power of the will to endure the hardships of the real world. But Reason, which demands the allegiance of all who would be sane, is to Lucy a grim deity who can offer her nothing but a prophecy of pain: "according to her, I was born only to work for a piece of bread, to await the pains of death, and steadily through all life to despond." "Vindictive as a devil . . . , envenomed as a step-mother," Reason seems to Lucy to take a "terrible revenge" on those who "defy her . . . and give a truant hour to Imagination." Yet to this "hag," who "frostily touch[es] [*her*] ear with the chill blue lips of eld" (*V*, I, 289–90), Lucy forces herself to listen; and she believes that in the "vigorous and revengeful" stifling of illusory hope, Reason "did right" (*V*, II, 2).

The "bitter sternness" (*V*, I, 290) of the rational doctrine to which Lucy commits herself can, however, stifle neither her love for Dr. John nor the pain it produces. He is to her "as good . . . as the well is to the parched wayfarer—as the sun to the shivering jail-bird," (*V*, I, 313); and when for a time all communication with him ends, none of "the different expedients" with which she tries "to sustain and fill existence" are of any use: "the result was as if I had gnawed a file to satisfy hunger, or drank brine to quench thirst" (*V*, II, 20). Aware that she is powerless to make him love her, she forces herself to accept her sterile and lonely condition.

Reason may compel Lucy to give no outward sign of her misery, but reason is far from omnipotent: it is opposed not only by the bright angel Imagination, but also by the black demon Hypochondria, for whose victim the "solitary," "night . . . becomes an unkindly time[;] . . . sleep and his nature cannot agree: strange starts and struggles harass his couch; the sinister band of bad dreams . . . join league against him" (*V*, II, 19). The purely negative responses to which her rational faculty compels her to limit herself are, Lucy finds, in themselves the source of mental terrors: "The world can understand well enough the process of perishing for want of food: perhaps few persons can enter into or follow out that of

going mad from solitary confinement. They see the long-buried
prisoner disinterred, a maniac or an idiot!—how his senses left
him—how his nerves, first inflamed, underwent nameless agony,
and then sunk to palsy—is a subject too intricate for examination,
too abstract for popular comprehension" (V, II, 28).

Tutored by Reason and fearing the rebuff it predicts, she has
willingly disguised her real self from Dr. John and has believed that
"in quarters where we can never be rightly known, we take pleasure . . . in being consummately ignored" (V, I, 121). But as she
discovers, the disguise is all too effective; and his casual assumption
that she is just what she has appeared to be fills her with bitterness
because it not only reveals his lack of romantic interest in her to be
absolute but also indicates that even his friendship was offered not
to Lucy but to a being who does not exist:

> I smiled; but I also hushed a groan. Oh!—I wished he would just let me
> alone—cease allusion to me. These epithets—these attributes I put from
> me. His "quiet Lucy Snowe," his "inoffensive shadow," I gave him back;
> not with scorn, but with extreme weariness; theirs was the coldness and the
> pressure of lead; let him whelm me with no such weight. . . . He wanted
> always to give me a role not mine. . . . He did not at all guess what I felt: he
> did not read my eyes, or face, or gestures; though; I doubt not, all spoke.
> (V, II, 84–85)

Although Lucy's agony is the result not of any malevolent action
on the part of any one person but is solely the product of her own
responses to the situation in which she is placed, Charlotte insists
that Lucy's situation is in itself the result of perverse cultural attitudes which limit and repress women and that thus bring them
pain. In this society, only men have the power to chose their mates.
Paulina, despite her beauty and her wealth, forces herself to be
"dumb as the grave" about her growing love for Dr. John, for she is
too proud to risk being despised as she feels she would be "if [she]
failed in self-control, and whined out some rickety liking that was all
on [her] side" (V, II, 155). Lucy, in the midst of her heartbreak and
frustration, is still governed by the desire to retain some modicum of
self-respect; and thus she insists, "I disclaim, with the utmost scorn,
every sneaking suspicion of what are called 'warmer feelings;'
women do not entertain these 'warmer feelings' where, from the
commencement, through the whole progress of an acquaintance,

they have never once been cheated of the conviction that to do so would be to commit a mortal absurdity" (*V*, II, 2).

And Lucy, deprived by birth and circumstance, lacks all that could attract Dr. John: "In his victrix he required . . . the imprint of high cultivation, the consecration of careful and authoritative protection, the adjuncts that Fashion decrees, Wealth purchases, and Taste adjusts" (*V*, II, 151). Lucy, who has neither charm nor beauty and who must labor for her bread at a menial task, is an asexual being to him. His prescription to alleviate the distress of her "long-continued mental conflict" (*V*, I, 316) is cruelly imperceptive. He is no doubt right in saying "Happiness is the cure—a cheerful mind the preventive: cultivate both"; but as Lucy sadly remarks to herself, "No mockery in this world ever sounds to me so hollow as that of being told to *cultivate* happiness. What does such advice mean? Happiness is not a potato, to be planted in mould and tilled with manure. Happiness is a glory shining far down upon us out of Heaven" (*V*, I, 317).

A deeply passionate woman, Lucy is condemned to unhappiness and to a life of frustration because she does not conform to the pattern by which her society judges a woman's desirability. Although physical loveliness may not in itself be enough to win a husband, such attractiveness is considered to be essential to the female; and Lucy has "no beauty" (*V*, I, 182). Moreover, Dr. John's encomiums on Ginevra reveal that men judge women by even more stringent standards than beauty. Men, adamant in their wish to retain their position of dominance, demand that a truly feminine, virtuous woman give daily evidence of her emotional passivity and of her mental inferiority to, and total dependency upon, the males who govern her life.

Dr. John's attitudes are, therefore, typical: he falls in love with Ginevra, a mindless flirt, for having been smitten by her beauty, he assumes so seemingly ideal a creature must conform in all respects to his dream vision. Ginevra, who knows that "he thinks I am perfect" and admits that "one can't help, in his presence, rather trying to justify his good opinion," finds that "it does so tire one to be goody" (*V*, I, 111). She therefore treats him with indifferent coldness which, ironically enough, convinces him she is indeed an "angel" (*V*, I, 189). That he equates female virtue with lack of sexual response is clear, for when he sees Ginevra exchanging a passionate glance with a man she does love, he begins to despise her because he considers her response "neither girlish nor innocent"; and he asserts, "No woman, were she as beautiful as Aphrodite, who could give or receive such a glance, shall ever be sought in marriage by me" (V, I, 284).

Dr. John next turns his attention to Paulina Mary Home, who appears to be a child but is, in fact, a mature and passionate woman—and one willing to obey the rules of the game men ask her to play. Defining herself as "a thing double-existent—a child to . . . dear Papa, but no more a child to myself" (V, II, 156), she hides from her father the fact she has fallen in love because she fears that his discovery of her natural development will break his heart. Shrewdly aware that Dr. John will marry only a pure—by which he means sexually passive—woman, she sees the dangers in returning too "cordial" a response to his love letter. Consequently, as she tells Lucy, she "wrote [her answer] three times—chastening and subduing the phrases . . . till it seemed . . . to resemble a morsel of ice flavoured with ever so slight a zest of . . . sugar" (V, II, 158–59).

Paul Emanuel is led to a series of equally unrealistic and perverse assumptions about the female sex by his allegiance to the teachings of the Roman Catholic Church, which makes the natural inferiority of women a matter of doctrine. He firmly asserts that "women who are worthy of the name ought infinitely to surpass our coarse, fallible, self-indulgent sex, in the power to perform [charitable but unpleasant] duties" (V, I, 257). To him, a " 'woman of intellect,' . . . was a sort of 'lusus naturae,' a luckless accident, a thing for which there was neither place nor use in creation, wanted neither as wife nor worker. . . . He believed in his soul that lovely, placid, and passive feminine mediocrity was the only pillow on which manly thought and sense could find rest for its aching temples; and as to work, male mind alone could work to any practical result" (V, II, 131–32).

Therefore, despite the fact that Paul believes that Lucy Snowe is his soul mate—that she was "born under [his] star" and "where that is the case with mortals, the threads of their destinies are difficult to disentangle" (V, II, 148)—Paul fears and attempts to repress her passionate nature, which is like his own and which draws him to her. Convinced that her "triste, soumise, rêveuse" manner disguises a "sauvage" with "la flamme à l'âme" (V, II, 85), he insists that she has "need of a careful friend. . . . [Her] very faults imperatively require it. [She] want[s] so much checking, regulating, and keeping down"

(V, II, 142). Lucy understands what his fear demands that she become, and she bitterly rejects his attempts to make her conform to a pattern which she sees as perverse in itself and as antithetical to her own nature.

Finding her at an exhibition standing before a painting representing Cleopatra as a voluptuary, Paul immediately insists that Lucy examine instead a four-part series entitled "La vie d'une femme" which, while it defines the woman's life solely in terms of her sexual status, implies through both pose and setting that she is to remain sexually passive and that her emotions are to be turned into the safe channels of worship, maternal love, and grief. But as she obediently scans "these four 'Anges,' " Lucy finds herself rebelling against the assumption of the male-dominated society that a woman must be either a passionate fiend or a passionless saint. The " 'Jeune Fille,' coming out of a church-door," the " 'Mariée' with a long white veil, kneeling at a prie-dieu," the " 'Jeune Mère,' hanging disconsolate over a clayey and puffy baby," and the " 'Veuve,' . . . a black woman, . . . surveying an elegant French monument, set up in a corner of some Père la Chaise," were, Lucy says, "cold and vapid as ghosts," "insincere, ill-humoured, bloodless, brainless nonentities! As bad in their way as the indolent gipsy-giantess, the Cleopatra, in hers" (V, I, 255).

VI *Resignation, Acceptance, and Stoic Faith*

The first two volumes of the novel reveal that Lucy's frustration and agony are the products of intricately interwoven forces; the last volume describes her developing ability to change that which lies within her power and to accept without despair the miseries which she cannot escape. Lucy has been convinced from youth that happiness in this life is rare and reserved for those few beings particularly favored by God, and this belief remains as unchanged as her view that earthly bliss is not to be her portion. Her prediction that Paulina will continue to live a life of "promise, plan [and] harmony" is followed by her sad statement that "other lives [of which her own is one] run from the first another course" with "the sanction of God" (V, II, 160).

But while Lucy is no more hopeful than before of living a happy life, she no longer attempts to evade the suffering that she believes is in store for her, nor does she any longer try to suppress or ignore the pain she feels. Convinced that her suffering is part of God's plan for her, she faces the future with stoic faith and with the determination to act rather than to remain passive. But neither faith nor determination can alter Lucy's nature and situation. Despite her desire to find a new way to respond to experience, she cannot break her long-established habit of withdrawing when confronted with situations which require her to risk overt rebuff; and she remains burdened by her innate propensity to fear, anxiety, and sadness. The slow movement toward the moment when she avows and acts upon her love for Paul Emanuel reveals the agonizing difficulty of Lucy's battle with herself as again and again she urges herself to act and falls hopelessly back into passivity.

Lucy is beset by doubts born of her past disappointments. She also has reason to doubt, not Paul's love for her, but his willingness to commit himself to this love; for he, like her, is convinced that earthly life is a fleeting preparation for eternity and that God, who created and sustains the tiniest atom of life in His universe, demands that men submit their wills to His and accept the burden of sacrifice and suffering. The "self-denying and self-sacrificing part of the Catholic religion commanded the homage of his soul" (V, I, 257), and Paul's sincere desire to follow the teachings of the church impinge directly on his relationship with Lucy; for she is not only militantly committed to what he has been taught are the heretical doctrines of Protestantism but she also fails to conform to the pattern which Paul believes confers virtue upon the weak and erring female sex.

Lucy finds, therefore, that her deepest needs are thwarted not only by the defects of her own nature but also by the entire cultural tradition of the society in which she lives. She discovers that Paul has withdrawn from her upon the direction of his spiritual director to whom he has confessed his involvement in a "covenant of fraternity" with "a heretic": "I seemed to hear Père Silas annulling the unholy pact; warning his penitent of its perils; entreating, enjoining reserve, nay . . . commanding the enforcement of that new system whose frost had pierced to the marrow of my bones" (V, II, 209–10).

Having accepted the fact that Dr. John's overwhelming love for Paulina had erased even his slight concern for "quiet," "unobtrusive" Lucy Snowe from his mind, Lucy had earlier forced herself to accept the grief that came with her knowledge that "that goodly river . . . of whose waves a few reviving drops had trickled to my lips, was bending to another course [and] was leaving my little hut and field forlorn and sand-dry" (*V*, II, 54). Having believed that "if life be war, it seemed my destiny to conduct it single-handed" (*V*, II, 58,), she had earlier attempted to bury and forget her love, although "sometimes I thought the tomb unquiet, and dreamed strangely of disturbed earth, and of hair, still golden and living, obtruded through coffin-chinks" (*V*, II, 141). With Paul, she is again in danger of suffering from the agonies of unrequited love, but this time her rival is no mortal woman: it is his dead love, Justine Marie, who deprives Lucy of a place in Paul's heart. Dedicated to the belief that chastity purifies and that virginity sanctifies, the church directs Paul to deny his feeling for Lucy and to "worship" the memory of "his beloved saint" (*V*, II, 184), who in life conformed totally to the required pattern of passive innocence and who in death offers no threat to his celibate purity.

In a passage which brilliantly synthesizes the movement of the plot with its symbolic meaning, Lucy realizes that what endangers her hopes for happiness, her sanity, and her life itself is not the specter nun who has confronted her in the shadowy corridors and dark gardens of the Catholic school and who, she fears, "came out of [her] brain" (*V*, I, 316); her danger is the nun that haunts Paul's mind:

. . . as for Justine Marie, I knew what she was. . . . there were girls like her in Madame Beck's school—phlegmatics—pale, slow, inert, but kind-natured, neutral of evil, undistinguished for good.

If she wore angels' wings, I knew whose poet-fancy conferred them. If her forehead shone luminous with the reflex of a halo, I knew in the fire of whose irids that circlet of holy flame had generation.

Was I, then, to be frightened by Justine Marie? (*V*, II, 188)

Even if Justine is a creation of Paul's imagination, her power is nonetheless real; for Paul—who seems to be a "dévot qui n'ose pas bouger, à moins que son confesseur ne lui donne la permission" [pious little man who daren't move unless his confessor gives him permission] (*V*, II, 185) and who therefore demands of himself and his mate a purity which equates with sexual abstinence—may allow "the picture of a pale dead nun to rise, an eternal barrier," because she alone can satisfy "his heart, sworn to virginity" (*V*, II, 188).

Lucy is thus propelled toward an emotional and spiritual crisis: admitting to herself that she loves him but that he may yet be driven

by his sense of duty to leave her without a word, Lucy exists in
agony, enduring "blank yet burning days" (V, II, 246). "There
seems, to my memory, an entire darkness and distraction in some
certain minutes I then passed alone—a grief inexpressible over a
loss unendurable. *What* should I do: oh! *what* should I do; when all
my life's hope was thus torn by the roots out of my riven, outraged
heart?" (V, II, 249). She is placed on a "rack of pain . . . , driv-
en . . . almost into fever . . . [and] to the brink of frenzy" (V, II,
264). Feeling herself helpless, she does nothing but passively wait
for Paul to rescue her, although she wonders "could my Greatheart
overcome? Could my guide reach me?" (V, II, 250).

But Lucy is not destined to be rescued by another—she must
herself act. The excruciating pain she suffers becomes itself the
stimulus that rouses her and drives her, drugged and sick, from her
"dungeon" (V, II, 258): "To be still was not in my power, nor quietly
to observe" (V, II, 261). Finding Paul surrounded by the men and
women who would keep them separated, Lucy—who once felt it
would be better "to be dead," and who "studiously held the quick of
[her] nature" in "catalepsy" (V, I, 134)—now insists, "They out-
numbered me, and I was worsted and under their feet; but, as yet, I
was not dead" (V, II, 269). What she has feared has proved to be
true: for her to live *is* to suffer, to feel *is* to experience pain—but she
no longer attempts to escape from the only existence that is possible
for her:

The love, born of beauty was not mine: I had nothing in common with it: I
could not dare to meddle with it, but another love, venturing diffidently
into life after long acquaintance, furnace-tried by pain, stamped by con-
stancy, consolidated by affection's pure and durable alloy, submitted by
intellect to intellect's own tests, and finally wrought up, by his own process,
to his own unflawed completeness, this love that laughed at Passion, his fast
frenzies and his hot and hurried extinction, in *this* Love I had a vested
interest; and whatever tended either to its culture or its destruction I
could not view impassibly. (V, II, 279)

The climactic moment of her life has come when she must act in
an instant upon her declared belief that her sufferings are an integral
part of God's design for her life and that her life is itself but a
fragment of His perfect, coherent, universal plan. As Paul stands
before her, although his appearance gives no clue to his intentions,

she does not retreat from him but instead uses the moment to embrace the experience in all its pain:

If this were my last moment with him, I would not waste it in forced, unnatural distance. I loved him well—too well not to smite out of the path even Jealousy herself, when she would have obstructed a kind farewell. A cordial word from his lips, or a gentle look from his eyes, would do me good, for all the span of life that remained to me; it would be comfort in the last strait of loneliness; I would take it—I would taste the elixir, and pride should not spill the cup. . . . Pierced deeper than I could endure, made now to feel what defied suppression, I cried—
    "My heart will break!" (*V*, II, 294–95)

Although her spontaneous admission of her dependency on and her great need for him forces Paul to acknowledge the permanency of the bond between them, Lucy experiences no succeeding period of happiness. The momentary bliss of the knowledge that Paul loves her and intends to marry her is shadowed by his imminent departure on the journey from which he never returns. Recognizing his virtue and desirous of being only his "steward" (*V*, II, 307), of devoting her life to paying "homage" to this man who has become her "King" (*V*, II, 303) and her "Christian hero" (*V*, II, 188), she is compelled instead to live out her life alone. As Paul himself reminds her, "Miss Lucy must trust God and herself" (*V*, II, 305).

Paul's injunction summarizes the traditional Protestant doctrine that informs the novel.[6] Man is assured of nothing in this life but that he is subject to the will of a beneficent Creator who directs all to complete the pattern that He in His wisdom and love has ordained. For Paul and Lucy, there is no connubial happiness on earth: the God whom they both love and to whom they have both committed their erring souls with the prayer that He "be merciful to me, a sinner" (*V*, II, 219) unites them not in marriage but in the universal communion of suffering. They are, as Lucy asserts in her great paean of hard-won faith, fellow pilgrims in the journey that leads the wracked and riven soul from the temporal wilderness of pain home to eternal life: "His will be done, as done it surely will be, whether we humble ourselves to resignation or not. The impulse of creation forwards it; the strength of powers, seen and unseen, has its fulfilment in charge. . . . Let us so run that we may obtain; let us endure hardness as good soldiers; let us finish our course, and keep the faith, reliant in the issue to come off more than conquerors: 'Art thou not from everlasting mine Holy One? WE SHALL NOT DIE!' " (V, II, 240).

Though it has always been less popular than *Jane Eyre*, *Villette* is now generally considered to be Charlotte's finest work; for in this novel she displays an increased maturity of both thought and technique. This last completed book, in which Charlotte refashioned her traumatic Brussels experience in terms of her later life, provides preeminent evidence of the truth of Lord David Cecil's assertion that "it is the fact . . . that her passion is enrolled in the service of a severe moral philosophy that constitutes her individuality" and "power."[7]

After the publication of *Jane Eyre*, Charlotte assessed *The Professor*, and concluded that the "whole narrative was deficient in incident."[8] In *Villette*, she removed this deficiency, introducing drama and excitement by using and intensifying the mode of *Jane Eyre*. By limiting the point of view to that of a highly sensitive woman dominated by an obsessive imagination, Charlotte gained access to a varied store of powerfully evocative images. Lucy longs to return to the passive routine of Madame Beck's school "as the criminal on the scaffold longs for the axe to descend" (V, I, 287); and when she enters the building, she feels as if "the axe had fallen" (V, I, 289). To her, the severe and demanding Mr. Paul, who watches her struggle with difficult lessons, "follow[s] footprints that . . . were sometimes marked in blood—follow[s] them grimly, holding the austerest police-watch over the pain-pressed pilgrim" (V, II, 126).

Unlike *Shirley*, *Villette* is devoid of explicit comment on social issues; what might be termed the public themes of the deficiencies of Roman Catholicism and the repression of women are presented only as aspects of Lucy Snowe's personal experience. They thus have immediate aesthetic significance, for they contribute at once to our knowledge both of the cause and the degree of Lucy's suffering, which is the major theme of the novel.

Villette is an extended study of what in his study of Charlotte's use of "new Gothic," R. B. Heilman calls "psychic darkness."[9] Unlike the protagonists of eighteenth-century picaresque novels, Lucy is bound upon a journey of discovery not of the outer world but of her own inner nature. Matthew Arnold in his poem "The Buried Life" (1852) expresses an idea of increasingly disturbing interest to his contemporaries when he speaks of how Fate "Bade through the deep recesses of our breast/ The unregarded river of our life / Pursue with indiscernible flow its way." *Villette* is centrally concerned with this theme of the dark, powerful, uncontrolled self that lies beneath the social facade.

In all of Charlotte's work, the concept of the many-faceted self appears, but while her earlier protagonists take pride in their ability to cloak passion with impassive respectability and to gain relief from frustrating reality in fiery dream, Lucy finds not only that wish-fulfilling fantasy is insufficient to sustain life but also that her imagination is the source of pain and fear as well as of pleasure. Fearful that by having indulged in the "necromantic joys of fancy" (V, I, 93) she has become the prey of spontaneous delusion, Lucy stares with horror at the figure of the nun, wondering whether "that strange thing was of this world, or of a realm beyond the grave; or whether indeed it was only the child of malady, and I of that malady the prey" (V, I, 319). The fact that what she sees is ultimately revealed to be only a roué in disguise is finally unimportant; for it is not the melodramatic cause but the quality of Lucy's reaction that signifies. And her intuitive association of her own imprisoned life with the story of a girl buried alive for breaking the vows of her order, makes the gloomy apparition the symbol of both her sterile present and her hopeless future.

Unlike *Jane Eyre*, *Villette* offers no wish-fulfilling solutions to either heroine or reader. Forcing herself to write while struggling daily with anguish over the loss of her sisters, Charlotte expressed not only her own pain and despair in Lucy's story but also her stubborn and sustaining belief in Christianity. Neither supernatural nor human agency offers Lucy an anodyne for suffering. Her "Greatheart" and "Champion" is swallowed by the tempestuous sea, and Lucy is again left alone to confront both a hostile world and the "Apollyon" of her mental terrors (V, II, 250). She is more akin to a tormented Job than to a Cinderella, and like Charlotte, she survives by accepting the extremity of ceaseless pain, remaining the while unshaken in the belief that "amidst His boundless works, is somewhere stored the secret of this last fate's justice: I know that His treasures contain the proof as the promise of its mercy" (V, II, 160).

CHAPTER 7

Assessing the Achievement

WITH the publication of *Jane Eyre*, Charlotte Brontë achieved immediate success. Her publisher, George Smith, found the work so fascinating that in order to finish reading it he canceled an appointment and bolted his dinner;[1] and his response was not unusual. As Kathleen Tillotson points out in *Novels of the Eighteen-Forties*, the book immediately became a subject of enthusiastic discussion among the novel-reading public.[2] One of the earliest reviews, by no less influential a critic than G. H. Lewes, set the tone of much that was to follow. Asserting that *Jane Eyre* "is a book after our own heart," he praised its then unknown author: "almost all that we require in a novelist she has: perception of character, and power of delineating it; picturesqueness; passion; and knowledge of life." He considered that the "charm" of the book inhered in the fact that "it is soul speaking to soul; it is an utterance from the depths of a struggling, suffering, much-enduring spirit: *suspiria de profundis.*" Lewes climaxed his review by calling attention to the novel's remarkable realism: "This faculty for objective representation is also united to a strange power of subjective representation. We do not simply mean the power over the passions—the psychological intuition of the artist, but the power also of connecting external appearances with internal effects—of representing the psychological interpretation of material phenomena."[3]

The contemporary view of Charlotte's work was not, of course, totally laudatory: her subject matter and her technique were both attacked. A segment of the public followed the lead of those reviewers who defined *Jane Eyre* as an "anti-Christian composition,"[4] a work that "burns with moral Jacobinism";[5] and consequently, to Charlotte's pain, this novel gained the reputation in some circles of being a "naughty book."[6] Charlotte was also accused of aesthetic deficiencies by G. H. Lewes in his review of *Shirley*, which he described as being "not a picture but a portfolio of random sketches," a work in which "all unity is wanting."[7] And the powerful emotion which informs *Villette* made that novel distasteful to many. To Thackeray, it was "an excellently written book . . . but a very disagreeable one. [Miss Brontë] turns everyone seamy side out."[8] Matthew Arnold remarked that "Miss Brontë has written a hideous, undelightful, convulsed, constricted novel . . . one of the most utterly disagreeable books I have ever read,"[9] and he considered the fault of the work to lie in the fact that "the writer's mind contains nothing but hunger, rebellion and rage and therefore that is all she can, in fact, put into her book."[10]

But even these negative observations bear witness to the fact that eminent literary figures believed Charlotte Brontë important enough to merit serious consideration. And balancing these adverse comments are others, such as that made by Lewes, who considered *Villette* "a work of astonishing power and passion."[11] This view is expressed even more strongly by George Eliot, who felt *Villette* to be "a still more wonderful book than *Jane Eyre*. There is something almost preternatural in its power."[12]

While the response of twentieth-century critics is also mixed, Charlotte Brontë's continuing popular appeal is, in itself, an indication of her achievement. Today, no study of the English novel is complete without a commentary on her work; and although her style and inability to plot are frequently criticized, to such modern scholars as David Daiches, Richard Chase, and R. B. Heilman, her novels bear the authentic stamp of genius in that they are pioneering and powerful explorations of the hidden facets of the human psyche. Charlotte herself both defined and accepted the limits of her range when, in the first days of her association with her publishers, she warned them that they must not expect her to be prolific:

Details, situations which I do not understand and cannot personally inspect, I would not for the world meddle with. . . . Besides, not one feeling on any subject, public or private, will I ever affect that I do not really experience. Yet though I must limit my sympathies; though my observation cannot penetrate where the very deepest political and social truths are to be learnt; though many doors of knowledge which are open for you are for ever shut to me; though I must guess and calculate and grope my way in the dark, and come to uncertain conclusions unaided and alone where such writers as Dickens and Thackeray, having access to the shrine and image of Truth,

have only to go into the temple, lift the veil a moment, and come out and
say what they have seen—yet with every disadvantage, I mean still, in my
own contracted way, to do my best. Imperfect my best will be, and poor,
and compared with the works of the true masters . . . it will be trifling, but
I trust not affected or counterfeit.[13]

This conviction that an artist must abide by the restrictions imposed
by inner nature led her to take an excessively moderate view of her
achievement. *Villette,* she rather sadly remarked, "touches on no
matter of public interest. I cannot write books handling the topics of
the day; it is of no use trying. Nor can I write a book for its moral.
Nor can I take up a philanthropic scheme. . . . "[14] Yet she asserted
to Harriet Martineau, "better the highest part of what is in your own
self than all the political and religious controversy in the world."[15]
And when, contending that literature should serve a social purpose,
Martineau attacked *Villette* on the grounds that she did "not like the
love, either the kind or degree of it,"[16] because it was psychologically inaccurate to write of "female characters . . . [whose] thoughts
and lives are full of one thing . . . love,"[17] Charlotte heatedly denied that she had created a work which was untrue to reality and
defended the territory she had marked out as her own: "I know what
love is as I understand it; and if man or woman should be ashamed of
feeling such love, then is there nothing right, noble, faithful, truthful, unselfish in this earth, as I comprehend rectitude, nobleness,
fidelity, truth, and disinterestedness."[18]

Charlotte's analysis of her capacities and achievement is accurate:
her province is not the social world but the heart and mind. That her
sincerity led to bigotry in her treatment of religion, that her experience and shyness condemned her to parodic imitation in her handling of the manners and conversation of the socially powerful, and
that her desire to satisfy the "passionate [public] preference for the
wild, wonderful, and thrilling," as she noted in her preface to *The
Professor,* resulted in her use of melodramatic incident, is un-
doubted. But no less obvious is the fact that despite these flaws, her
novels brought something new to the tradition of the English novel.
Walter Allen's assertion that she depicts "the isolated, naked
soul responding to the experience of life with a maximum of intensity"[19] confirms her success in meeting the standard she had set
for herself when, urged by her publishers to quickly repeat the success of *Jane Eyre,* she announced, "unless I have something of my

own to say, and a way of my own to say it in, I have no business to publish."[20]

Her achievement is amazing, since perhaps no other writer committed to speaking only of self-tested experience has worked with less immediately promising material than did Charlotte Brontë, whose severely limited life deprived her not only of intimate knowledge of the great events of her times but even of ordinary social intercourse. Charlotte lived the greater part of her existence within the confines of her family; and as that family dwindled, she found herself cast back more and more upon her own resources. Burdened by excessive shyness, bound by a sense of her father's need, she was unable to enter London's literary salons even when their doors stood open to receive her. The picture of her lonely existence presented to us by Mrs. Gaskell conveys not only literal fact but symbolic meaning:

For as long as I can remember—Tabby says since they were little "bairns—Miss Brontë & Miss Emily & Miss Anne used to put away their sewing after prayers & walk all three one after the other round the table in the parlour till near eleven o'clock. Miss Emily walked as long as she could, & when she died Miss Anne & Miss Brontë took it up,—and now my heart aches to hear Miss Brontë walking, walking, on alone." And on enquiring I found that after Miss Brontë had seen me to my room she did come down every night, & begin that slow monotonous incessant walk in which I am sure I should fancy I heard the steps of the dead following me. She says she could not sleep without it—that she and her sisters talked over the places & projects of their whole lives at such times.[21]

As Charlotte struggled against grief and loneliness, the parsonage, which had become both prison and refuge, may indeed have seemed to her to be peopled with the specters of the dead; but it also held other phantoms—there she fought the demon-hag hypochondria; there she found herself torn between the blandishments of the "good angel" Imagination and the stern warnings of "envenomed" Reason. And this intense inner life she turned into fiction. Her protagonists are all aspects of herself, studies in frustrated energy who, deprived by personality, conscience, and circumstance of the life of fire and feeling they both desire and fear, turn inward, doing battle with their own ambivalent emotions, taking every external event as an ominous indication of a fate to be suffered, a punishment to be endured.

Indeed, Charlotte Brontë's real power lies in her ability to portray minds that internalize all experience; the atmosphere of almost frenetic action that pervades her novels stems not so much from dramatic events as from the metaphoric language that describes the excited agony of the internal struggle that goes on ceaselessly under a placid exterior. Jane Eyre, sitting ignored in the Thornfield drawing room, is penetrated by "a steely point of agony"; Caroline, forcing herself to admit that Robert will show no interest in her, describes her mental anguish by saying that she must close her hand upon a scorpion; Lucy, sure that Paul will never declare his love, "invok[es] conviction to nail upon [her] the certainty abhorred while embraced, to fix it with the strongest spikes her strongest strokes could drive."

Charlotte's great theme is the search for love. In *The Professor*, her first adult novel, published last and posthumously, we see the author break away from her earlier fantasies to write of real men and women. In this novel, Charlotte emphasizes her hero's confusion as he attempts to distinguish appearances from reality, to distinguish between his own conflicting motives, and to control opposed impulses by force of will. In *Jane Eyre*, her second novel, Charlotte dips back into her adolescent fantasies, yet even in doing so, she does not surrender her informing awareness that the very complexity of her heroine's motives helps to account for the confusion and fear she feels as she searches for her soul mate in an inimical society. If in *Jane Eyre*, Charlotte expresses fantasies which every woman recognizes from her own adolescence, in *Shirley*, the closest she comes to writing a thesis novel, Charlotte illuminates and criticizes the social attitudes which drive women—starved for economic security and social identity—to such fantasies. *Shirley* is the first major novel of the feminist movement. It is still one of the best. Finally, in *Villette*, Charlotte brings together the achievements of her earlier three novels. We return to *Jane Eyre* for pleasurable release; we return to *Villette*, Charlotte's great masterpiece, for tragic catharsis—the purging of pity and fear. *Villette* is a book of triumph in despair. In *Jane Eyre*, the heroine may renounce the requirements of a rigorous Christianity which calls upon her to reject the love of her heart, Rochester. In *Villette*, Lucy Snowe, though she is doomed to a life of suffering, asserts and accepts the belief that her personal tragedy is part of God's mysterious but perfect plan.

Drawn from the deep well of her own tortured consciousness, Charlotte Brontë's fiction has a universal quality not only because of the power of her expression but also because the emotions she felt in extreme degree are universal ones: she is the poet of the troubled reaches of the mind, of the imagination, and of the subconscious. To read her work is, therefore, to be cast into the phantasmagoric world created by the agonized mind driven to the verge of despair; and the "preternatural" power of her fiction derives from the fact that Charlotte Brontë did indeed "have something of [her] own to say." Forced to endure great grief, frustrated in her deepest desires during most of her life, afraid of the imaginative power that was also her greatest solace, she wrought from the materials of her tragic life the novels which give a new dimension to her readers' understanding of the human heart.

Notes and References

Chapter One

1. David Cecil, *Victorian Novelists: Essays in Revaluation* (1935; reprint ed., Chicago, 1958), p. 103.
2. John Lock and Canon W. T. Dixon, *A Man of Sorrows* (London, 1965), pp. 7–13.
3. Lock and Dixon, p. 240.
4. Elizabeth Gaskell, *The Life of Charlotte Brontë* (1857; reprint ed., Edinburgh, 1924), pp. 38, 40.
5. Lock and Dixon, p. 253.
6. Winifred Gérin, *Charlotte Brontë: The Evolution of Genius* (Oxford, 1967), p. 23.
7. Gérin, p. 23.
8. Gérin, p. 6.
9. Gaskell, p. 58.
10. Gérin, p. 14.
11. Gérin, p. 15.
12. Gérin, p. 16.
13. E. M. Delafield, *The Brontës: Their Lives Recorded by Their Contemporaries* (London, 1935), p. 25.
14. Gérin, p. 11.
15. Gaskell, p. 105.
16. Delafield, p. 35.
17. Gérin, p. 14.
18. Delafield, p. 35.
19. Delafield, p. 40.
20. Delafield, p. 54.
21. *The Brontës: Their Lives, Friendships and Correspondence in Four Volumes*, ed. T. J. Wise and J. A. Symington (Oxford, 1932), I, 129; cited below as *Life and Letters*.
22. Fannie E. Ratchford, *The Brontë's Web of Childhood* (1941; reissued, New York, 1964), p. 67.
23. Ratchford, p. 105.

24. Gérin, pp. 103–04.
25. *Life and Letters*, I, 155.
26. *Life and Letters*, I, 137.
27. *Life and Letters*, I, 143.
28. *Life and Letters*, I, 139.
29. Gérin, pp. 105–06.
30. Gérin, p. 141.
31. Gérin, p. 113.
32. *Life and Letters*, I, 226.
33. *Life and Letters*, I, 241.
34. *Life and Letters*, I, 260.
35. *Life and Letters*, I, 297.
36. *Life and Letters*, II, 3.
37. *Life and Letters*, II, 53–54.
38. *The Miscellaneous and Unpublished Writings of Charlotte and Patrick Branwell Brontë in Two Volumes*, ed. T. J. Wise and J. A. Symington (Oxford, 1938), II, 404.
39. Ratchford, p. 163.
40. *Life and Letters*, II, 115.
41. *Life and Letters*, II, 13.
42. Gérin, p. 322.
43. Gérin, p. 337.
44. Gérin, p. 340.
45. *Life and Letters*, II, 289.
46. *Life and Letters*, II, 293.
47. *Life and Letters*, II, 294.
48. *Life and Letters*, II, 301.
49. *Life and Letters*, II, 295.
50. *Life and Letters*, II, 299–301.
51. *Life and Letters*, III, 6.
52. *Life and Letters*, III, 246.
53. *Life and Letters*, IV, 6.
54. *Life and Letters*, IV, 18.
55. Gérin, p. 494.
56. *Life and Letters*, IV, 119.
57. *Life and Letters*, IV, 29.
58. *Life and Letters*, IV, 57.
59. *Life and Letters*, I, 174.
60. *Life and Letters*, IV, 167.
61. Ratchford, pp. 185–87.
62. Gaskell, p. 523.

Chapter Two

1. *The Poems of Charlotte Brontë and Patrick Branwell Brontë*, ed. T. J. Wise and J. A. Symington (Oxford, 1934), p. 186.

2. *The Miscellaneous and Unpublished Writings of Charlotte and Patrick Branwell Brontë in Two Volumes*, ed. T. J. Wise and J. A. Symington (Oxford, 1938), I, 278–79; hereafter cited as *MUW*.

3. *Legends of Angria*, ed. Fannie Ratchford and William Clyde DeVane (New Haven, 1933), p. 65; hereafter cited as *LA*.

4. Ratchford, p. 45.

5. *Five Novelettes*, ed. Winifred Gérin (London, 1971), p. 127; hereafter cited as *FN*.

6. Ratchford, pp. 142–43.

7. Ratchford, pp. 113–14.

8. *Shirley*, 2 vols. (Oxford, 1931), II, 256.

Chapter Three

1. *The Professor* (Oxford, 1931), p. 3; hereafter cited as *P*.

2. W. A. Craik, *The Brontë Novels* (1968; reprint ed., London, 1971), p. 48.

3. Robert Bernard Martin, *The Accents of Persuasion: Charlotte Brontë's Novels* (London, 1966), p. 28.

Chapter Four

1. G. Armour Craig, "The Unpoetic Compromise: On the Relation Between Private Vision and Social Order in Nineteenth-Century Fiction," in *Self and Society in the Novel*, ed. Mark Schorer (New York, 1956), p. 40.

2. *Jane Eyre*, 2 vols. (Oxford, 1931), I, 59; hereafter cited as *JE*.

3. Richard Chase, "The Brontës, or Myth Domesticated" in *Forms of Modern Fiction*, ed. William Van O'Connor (Bloomington, 1959), p. 108; M. H. Scargill, "All Passion Spent: A Revaluation of *Jane Eyre*," *University of Toronto Quarterly*, 19 (January, 1950), 22–23.

4. R. E. Hughes, "Jane Eyre: The Unbaptized Dionysos," *Nineteenth Century Fiction*, 18 (March, 1964), 347–64.

5. Robert B. Heilman, "Charlotte Brontë, Reason and the Moon," *Nineteenth Century Fiction*, 14 (March, 1960), 283–302.

6. [Elizabeth Rigby], "*Vanity Fair*—and *Jane Eyre*," *The Quarterly Review*, 84 (1848–1849), 173. This unsigned review is generally attributed to Elizabeth Rigby.

7. Delafield, p. 55.

Chapter Five

1. Kathleen Tillotson, *Novels of the Eighteen-Forties* (1956; reprint ed., London, 1961), pp. 78–87.

2. *Life and Letters*, II, 216.

3. Ivy Holgate, "The Structure of *Shirley*," *Brontë Society Transactions*, 14 (1962), 27–35.

4. *Shirley*, 2 vols. (Oxford, 1931), I, 29–30; hereafter cited as *S*.

5. In her May 12, 1848, letter to Wi'liam Smith Williams, Charlotte

discusses the unhappy condition of most women and makes this link apparent by saying, "when patience has done its utmost and industry its best, whether in the case of women or operatives, and when both are baffled, and pain and want triumph, the sufferer is free, is entitled, at last to send up to Heaven any piercing cry for relief, if by that cry he can hope to obtain succour" *(Life and Letters,* II, 216).

6. [George Henry Lewes], from an unsigned review in *Edinburgh Review,* 91 (January, 1850) 153–73; reprinted in *The Brontës: The Critical Heritage,* ed. Miriam Allott (Boston, 1974), p. 164.

Chapter Six

1. *Villette,* 2 vols. (Oxford, 1931), II, 58; hereafter cited as *V.*
2. Philip Momberger, "Self and World in the Works of Charlotte Brontë," *English Literary History,* 32 (September, 1965), 349–55.
3. *Life and Letters,* II, 338.
4. *Life and Letters,* IV, 18.
5. Heilman, "Charlotte Brontë, Reason, and the Moon," pp. 283–88.
6. Martin, p. 145.
7. Cecil, p. 123.
8. *Life and Letters,* II, 161.
9. R. B. Heilman, "Charlotte Brontë's New Gothic," in *From Jane Austen to Joseph Conrad,* ed. Robert C. Rathburn and Martin Steinmann, Jr. (Minneapolis, 1958), p. 119.

Chapter Seven

1. George Smith, "Charlotte Brontë," *The Cornhill Magazine,* 9 (December, 1900), 782.
2. *Novels of the Eighteen-Forties,* p. 258.
3. George Henry Lewes, "Recent Novels: English and French," *Fraser's Magazine,* 36 (December, 1847), 691, 693.
4. [Rigby], p. 173.
5. From an unsigned review in *The Christian Remembrancer,* 10 (April, 1848), 397.
6. George Smith recounted how, on the occasion of their first meeting, G. H. Lewes leaned across the dinner table and said, "There ought to be a bond of sympathy between us, Miss Brontë, for we have both written naughty books." A friend of Smith's mother remarked on seeing a copy of *Jane Eyre,* "You surely do not leave such a book as *this* about, at the risk of your daughter reading it" (Smith, p. 792).
7. Lewes, in *The Brontës: The Critical Heritage,* p. 165.
8. *The Letters and Private Papers of William Makepeace Thackeray,* ed. Gordon S. Ray, 4 vols. (Cambridge, 1946), III, 321.
9. *Letters of Matthew Arnold to Hugh Clough,* ed. Howard Foster Lowry (Oxford, 1968), letter number 43.

10. *Letters of Matthew Arnold 1848–1888*, ed. G. W. E. Russell, 2 vols. (London, 1895), I, 29.

11. *"Ruth* and *Villette,"* *Westminster Review*, 59 (April, 1853), 485.

12. *The George Eliot Letters*, ed. G. S. Haight, 6 vols. (New Haven, 1954), II, 87.

13. *Life and Letters*, II, 184.

14. *Life and Letters*, IV, 14.

15. *Life and Letters*, III, 303.

16. *Life and Letters*, IV, 41.

17. From an unsigned review in *Daily News*, February 3, 1853; reprinted in *The Brontës: The Critical Heritage*, p. 172.

18. *Life and Letters*, IV, 42.

19. Walter Allen, *The English Novel* (1954; reprint ed., New York, 1958), p. 222.

20. *Life and Letters*, II, 255.

21. Clement Shorter, "Introduction," *The Life of Charlotte Brontë*, by Elizabeth Gaskell (1857; reprint ed., New York, 1951), p. xiv.

Selected Bibliography

The following bibliography is selective. Only the most important biographical sources are listed, but an attempt has been made to cite all significant critical articles.

PRIMARY SOURCES

1. Collected Editions
The Shakespeare Head Brontë. Edited by T. J. Wise and J. A. Symington. 19 vols. Oxford: The Shakespeare Head Press, 1931–1938. Most reliable and complete collection of the primary material: novels, 11 vols.; life and letters, 4 vols.; poems, 2 vols.; miscellaneous and unpublished writings, 2 vols.
Five Novelettes. Edited by Winifred Gérin. London: The Folio Press, 1971.
Legends of Angria. Edited by Fannie E. Ratchford and William Clyde DeVane. New Haven: Yale University Press, 1933.
The Twelve Adventurers and Other Stories. Edited C. K. Shorter [and C. W. Hatfield]. London: Hodder and Stoughton, 1925.

2. Individual Works
Jane Eyre, An Autobiography. "Edited by Currer Bell." 3 vols. London: Smith, Elder and Company, 1847.
Shirley, A Tale. 3 vols. London: Smith, Elder and Company, 1849.
Villette. 3 vols. London: Smith, Elder and Company, 1853.
The Professor, A Tale. 2 vols. London: Smith, Elder and Company, 1857.

SECONDARY SOURCES

1. Bibliography
PASSEL, ANNE. "Charlotte Brontë: A Bibliography of the Criticism of Her Novels." *Bulletin of Bibliography and Magazine Notes,* 26 (October–December, 1969), 118–20; 27 (January–March, 1970), 13–20.

2. Biography
DELAFIELD, E. M. *The Brontës: Their Lives Recorded by Their Contemporaries.* London: Hogarth Press, 1935. Contemporary descriptions of the Brontës by those who knew or saw them.

GASKELL, E[LIZABETH] C. *The Life of Charlotte Brontë.* Edinburgh: John Grant, 1924. First and still the basic biographical study.

GÉRIN, WINIFRED. *Charlotte Brontë: The Evolution of Genius.* Oxford: Oxford University Press, Clarendon Press, 1967. Definitive modern biography.

LOCK, JOHN, and CANON W. T. DIXON. *A Man of Sorrows: The Life, Letters and Times of the Rev. Patrick Brontë 1777–1861.* London: Thomas Nelson and Sons, 1965. Contains valuable information on church politics.

SMITH, GEORGE. "Charlotte Brontë." *The Cornhill Magazine,* 9 (December, 1900), 778–95. Personal reminiscence.

3. Criticism

ALLEN, WALTER. *The English Novel.* 1954; reprinted New York: Dutton, 1958. Provides a short critical commentary on the work of Brontë in relation to the main stream of the English novel.

ALLOTT, MIRIAM, ed. *The Brontës; The Critical Heritage.* Boston: Routledge & Kegan Paul, 1974. Reprints significant nineteenth-century criticism of the Brontës; provides a long introductory chapter which synthesizes these responses.

BLOM, M. A. "Apprenticeship in 'the World Below': Charlotte Brontë's *Juvenilia.*" *English Studies in Canada,* 1 (Fall, 1975), 280–303. A critical study of the juvenilia.

———. "Charlotte Brontë, Feminist *Manquée.*" *Bucknell Review,* 21 (Spring, 1973), 87–102. Discusses Charlotte Brontë's ambivalent attitude to the roles women are asked to play in male-dominated society.

———. "*Jane Eyre:* Mind as Law Unto Itself." *Criticism,* 15 (Fall, 1973), 350–64. Argues that in crises, Jane rejects society's dictates and acts in terms of her own beliefs and needs.

BRIGGS, ASA. "Private and Social Themes in *Shirley.*" *Brontë Society Transactions,* 13 (1958), 203–19. Suggests there are three themes in "the first impressive regional novel in the English language."

BURKHART, CHARLES. "Another Key Word for *Jane Eyre.*" *Nineteenth Century Fiction,* 16 (1961), 177–79. Studies the use of the word "nature" as a guide to understanding the conflict in the novel.

———. "Brontë's *Villette.* *Explicator,* 21 (September, 1962), item 8. Views *Villette* as "an organic poetic metaphor"; discusses moon imagery.

CECIL, DAVID. *Victorian Novelists: Essays in Revaluation.* 1936; reprinted Chicago: University of Chicago Press, 1958. Sees the unique power of Charlotte's novels as arising from her own passionate inner life.

CHASE, RICHARD. "The Brontës, or Myth Domesticated." In *Forms of Modern Fiction,* edited by William Van O'Connor, pp. 102–19, Bloomington: University of Indiana Press, 1959. Examines *Wuthering Heights* and *Jane Eyre* in terms of the use they make of the "mythical, tragic point of view."

COLBY, ROBERT A. "*Villette* and the Life of the Mind." *Publications of the Modern Language Association,* 74 (September, 1960), 410–19. Approaches *Villette* as Charlotte Brontë's "literary, not . . . literal biography" and focuses on how Lucy moves from vicariously experiencing life through literature and art to actual involvement.

CRAIG, G. ARMOUR. "The Unpoetic Compromise: On the Relation Between Private Vision and Social Order in Nineteenth-Century English Fiction." In *Self and Society in the Novel,* edited by Mark Schorer, pp. 30–41. New York: Columbia University Press, 1956. Argues that "Jane Eyre's vision masters her world, but the price of her mastery is absolute isolation."

CRAIK, W. A. *The Brontë Novels.* 1968; reprinted London: Methuen, 1971. Considers the themes and techniques of the Brontë sisters' novels; places them in the contemporary context.

DAY, MARTIN S. "Central Concepts of *Jane Eyre.*" *The Personalist,* 61 (1960), 495–505. Discusses what Jane seeks in a mate.

DUNBAR, GEORGIA S. "Proper Names in *Villette.*" *Nineteenth Century Fiction,* 15 (June, 1960), 77–80. Suggests that the obvious appropriateness of the proper names reveals Charlotte's craftsmanship.

ERICKSEN, DONALD H. "Imagery as Structure in *Jane Eyre.*" *Victorian Newsletter,* no. 30 (1966), pp. 18–22. Argues that nature imagery reveals the "amatory element" in *Jane Eyre.*

EWBANK, INGA-STINA. *Their Proper Sphere: A Study of the Brontë Sisters as Early Victorian Novelists.* London: Edward Arnold, 1966. Analyzes the Brontës' handling of materials which women writers of the time were generally prohibited from using.

FALCONER, J. A. "*The Professor* and *Villette:* A Study of Development." *English Studies,* 9 (April, 1927), 33–37. Examines the two works in terms of the author's life.

GRIBBLE, JENNIFER. "Jane Eyre's Imagination." *Nineteenth Century Fiction,* 23 (December, 1968), 279–93. Discusses Jane's creative imagination, which transforms or appropriates "aspects of the natural world which it seizes as relevant."

HAGEN, JOHN. "Enemies of Freedom in *Jane Eyre.*" *Criticism,* 13 (Winter, 1971), 351–76. Examines Jane's various attempts to gain the freedom entailed in the ability to balance the claims of human and divine love.

HARDY, BARBARA. *The Appropriate Form: An Essay on the Novel.* London: Athlone Press, 1964. Sees *Jane Eyre* as shaped by "the dogmatism of a special belief, the belief in Providence."

HEILMAN, ROBERT B. "Charlotte Brontë's New Gothic." In *From Jane Austen to Joseph Conrad,* edited by Robert C. Rathburn and Martin Steinmann, Jr., pp. 118–32. Minneapolis: University of Minnesota Press, 1958. Suggests that Charlotte's exploration of "the dark side of feeling and personality" turns the Gothic tradition to new and original purposes.

————. "Charlotte Brontë, Reason, and the Moon." *Nineteenth Century Fiction*, 14 (March, 1960), 283–302. Examines Charlotte's use of the moon to illuminate the conflict between reason and imagination.

HOLGATE, IVY. "*Shirley:* Charlotte's Own Evidence." *Brontë Society Transactions*, 14 (1963), 27–35. Argues that on her own initiative Charlotte decided to treat the Luddite riots rather than Chartism.

————. "The Structure of Shirley." *Brontë Society Transactions*, 14 (1962), 27–35. Argues that Charlotte originally intended to deal with Chartism in contemporary Yorkshire.

HUGHES, R. "Jane Eyre: The Unbaptized Dionysos." *Nineteenth Century Fiction*, 18 (March, 1964), 347–64. Sees *Jane Eyre* as a religious novel in which Jane embodies the elemental conflict between Dionysos and Apollo.

JEFFARES, A. NORMAN. "*Shirley*—A Yorkshire Novel." *Brontë Society Transactions*, 15 (1969), 281–93. Discusses the regionalism of *Shirley;* comments on the novel's handling of "the plight of intelligent women."

JOHNSON, E. D. H. "Daring the Dread Glance: Charlotte Brontë's Treatment of the Supernatural in *Villette*." *Nineteenth Century Fiction*, 20 (March, 1966), 325–36. Argues that the novel has a four-part structure and that the appearances of the "nun" indicate the stages in Lucy's progress toward "self-realization."

KNIES, EARL A. *The Art of Charlotte Brontë*. Athens, Ohio: Ohio University Press, 1969. Examines the development of technique; elaborate discussion of point of view.

————. "The 'I' of *Jane Eyre*." *College English*, 27 (April, 1966), 547–56. Defends the integrity of Charlotte Brontë's use of first-person narration.

KORG, JACOB. "The Problem of Unity in *Shirley*." *Nineteenth Century Fiction*, 12 (September, 1957), 125–36. Argues that the theme of "romantic egoism" unifies the book.

KRAMER, DALE. "Thematic Structure in *Jane Eyre*." *Papers on Language and Literature*, 4 (Summer, 1968), 288–98. Discusses the interrelationship of plot and the theme of Jane's "movement towards self-realization."

LANGFORD, THOMAS. "The Three Pictures of *Jane Eyre*," *Victorian Newsletter*, no. 31 (1967), pp. 47–48. Discusses the symbolic meaning of Jane's drawings.

LEDERER, CLARA. " 'Little God-Sister.' " *Nineteenth Century Fiction* [then called *The Trollopian*], 2 (December, 1947), 169–75. Discusses the biographical element in *Villette*.

LODGE, DAVID. "Fire and Eyre: Charlotte Brontë's War of Earthly Elements." In *The Brontë's: A Collection of Critical Essays*, edited by Ian Gregor, pp. 110–36. Englewood Cliffs, New Jersey: Prentice-Hall, 1970. Suggests that earth, water, air, fire, the sun, and the moon form a "system of 'objective correlatives' " which facilitates an examination of emotional life.

MARTIN, ROBERT BERNARD. *Accents of Persuasion: Charlotte Brontë's Novels.* London: Faber and Faber, 1966. Studies themes and techniques with emphasis on the relationship between "reality" and "truth."

MILLGATE, JANE. "Narrative Distance in *Jane Eyre:* The Relevance of the Pictures." *Modern Language Review,* 63 (1968), 315–19. Argues that Jane's pictures are indicative of the various stages of her emotional development.

MOMBERGER, PHILIP. "Self and World in the Works of Charlotte Brontë." *English Literary History,* 32 (September, 1965), 349–69. Argues that all of Charlotte's protagonists are outcasts with remarkably similar attitudes toward themselves and the exterior world.

MOSER, LAWRENCE E., S.J. "From Portrait to Person: A Note on the Surrealistic in *Jane Eyre.*" *Nineteenth Century Fiction,* 20 (December, 1965), 275–81. Discusses the symbolic significance of Jane's paintings.

PASSEL, ANNE. "The Three Voices of Charlotte Brontë's *Shirley.*" *Brontë Society Transactions,* 15 (1969), 323–26. Argues that the novel is a "highly organized three-voiced contrapuntal structure."

PETERS, MARGOT. *Charlotte Brontë: Style in the Novel.* Madison, Wisconsin: University of Wisconsin Press, 1973. Examines the prose style of the novels.

PRESCOTT, JOSEPH. "*Jane Eyre:* A Romantic Exemplum with a Difference." In *Twelve Original Essays on Great English Novels,* edited by Charles Shapiro. Detroit: Wayne State University Press, 1958. Discusses the erotic imagery in *Jane Eyre;* argues that its use reveals Charlotte's own sexual repression.

RATCHFORD, FANNIE ELIZABETH. *The Brontë's Web of Childhood.* New York: Columbia University Press, 1941; reissued, New York: Russell and Russell, 1964. Examines the Glasstown and Angrian materials; a basic study.

SCARGILL, M. H. "All Passion Spent: A Revaluation of *Jane Eyre.*" *University of Toronto Quarterly,* 19 (January, 1950), 120–25. Discusses the tension between reason and passion.

SCHREIBER, ANNETTE. "The Myth in Charlotte Brontë." *Literature and Psychology,* 18 (1968), 48–67. Discusses the myth of the "woman's search for a lover and a mate."

SHANNON, EDGAR F., Jr. "The Present Tense in *Jane Eyre.*" *Nineteenth Century Fiction,* 10 (September, 1955), 141–45. Discusses the shifts to the present tense and argues that these mark structural divisions.

SHAPIRO, ARNOLD. "In Defense of *Jane Eyre.*" *Studies in English Literature,* 8 (1968), 681–98. Argues that although *Jane Eyre* has elements of fantasy in it, it is concerned with real problems to which it offers real solutions: the novel consistently calls for "openness and freedom between individuals."

————. "Public Themes and Private Lives: Social Criticism in *Shirley*." *Papers on Language and Literature*, 4 (Winter, 1968), 74–84. Argues that the novel does have unity in that "the historical economic crises of the outer world are exactly reflected in the private crises of the characters."

SMITH, DAVID. "Incest Patterns in Two Victorian Novels." *Literature and Psychology*, 15 (Summer, 1965), 136–62. Discusses what he sees as a perverse father-daughter relationship between Rochester and Jane.

SOLOMON, ERIC. "*Jane Eyre*, Fire and Water." *College English*, 25 (1963), 215–17. Argues that fire and water imagery develops and sustains a tension between passion and reason.

TILLOTSON, KATHLEEN. *Novels of the Eighteen-Forties*. London: Oxford University Press, 1956. Discusses *Jane Eyre* in relationship to other novels of its time.

TOMPKINS, J. M. S. "Caroline Helstone's Eyes." *Brontë Society Transactions*, 14 (1961), 18–28. Argues that after Anne's death, Charlotte altered her conception of Caroline, whom she had come to identify much more closely with her sister.

WATSON, MELVIN R. "Form and Substance in the Brontë Novels." In *From Jane Austen to Joseph Conrad*, edited by Robert C. Rathburn and Martin Steinmann, Jr., pp. 106–17. Minneapolis: University of Minnesota Press, 1958. Argues that *Jane Eyre* is Charlotte's one successful novel because only in it are "form and substance blended."

Index

(The works of Charlotte Brontë are listed under her name)